TWENTY-FIRST CENTURY
WARSHIPS
SURFACE COMBATANTS OF TODAY'S NAVIES

TWENTY-FIRST CENTURY
WARSHIPS

SURFACE COMBATANTS OF TODAY'S NAVIES

Steve Crawford

Grange
BOOKS

This edition published in 2002 by Grange Books
Grange Books plc
The Grange
1–6 Kingsnorth Estate
Hoo
Near Rochester
Kent ME3 9ND

www.grangebooks.co.uk

© 2002 Brown Partworks Limited

ISBN 1-84013-496-8

Editorial and design:
Brown Partworks Limited
8 Chapel Place
Rivington Street
London
EC2A 3DQ
UK

Printed in Hong Kong

Editor: Peter Darman
Picture research: Andrew Webb
Design: Richard Berry
Production: Matt Weyland

CONTENTS

HMAS ANZAC

This Anzac class frigate is a joint Australia–New Zealand project for a total of 10 warships. The design is based on the Blohm & Voss Meko 200 modular design which utilizes a basic hull and construction concept to provide flexibility in the choice of command and control, weapons, equipment and sensors. The *Anzac* is armed with one eight-cell Mk 41 Vertical Launching System (VLS) for NATO Sea Sparrow surface-to-air missiles (SAMs). Sea Sparrow is a semi-active radar missile with a range of 14.5km (9 miles). The capacity to launch eight Boeing Harpoon anti-ship missiles (ASMs) is also to be added. The main gun is a United Defense 127mm Mk 45 Model 2, which can fire at a rate of 20 rounds a minute up to a range of 20km (12.43 miles). Two triple 324mm Mk 32 torpedo tubes for Mk 46 anti-submarine torpedoes are also fitted to the ship. The Mk 46 is an active/passive torpedo with a range of 11km (6.83 miles). This state-of-the-art frigate is equipped with a Sceptre A radar warner and will be fitted with a radar jammer which as yet does not have an official name. Decoy systems on the ship consist of Mk 36 launchers for Sea Gnat decoys and SLQ-25A towed torpedo decoys. Each ship is designed to accommodate, operate and maintain a Sikorsky S-70B2 helicopter, to be replaced later by the Kaman SH-2G Super Seasprite.

SPECIFICATIONS

Type:	frigate
Crew:	163
Displacement:	3658 tonnes (3600 tons)
Length:	118m (387.13ft)
Beam:	14.8m (48.55ft)
Draught:	4.35m (14.27ft)
Speed:	27 knots
Range:	9654km (6000 miles)
Missiles:	Sea Sparrow SAM, Harpoon ASM
Guns:	1 x 127mm
Torpedoes:	Mk 46
Helicopters:	1 x S-70B2
Aircraft:	none
Air Search Radar:	SPS-49 (V) 8
Surface Radar:	CelsiusTech 9LV 453 TIR
Fire Control Radar:	unknown
Propulsion:	2 x diesels, 30,000shp

COLOSSUS

An ex-Royal Navy light fleet carrier acquired in 1956, the *Colossus* is the Brazilian Navy's largest ship, and despite its considerable age, remains in service. She will be replaced by the *Sao Paulo* (the former French carrier acquired in 2000) and decommissioned by 2003. Originally built by Swan Hunter, it was laid down on 16 November 1942, launched on 23 February 1944 and commissioned on 15 January 1945. She served in the Mediterranean, then in the Pacific, participated in cold-weather trials in the Arctic in 1948–49, and served as a troop and aircraft transport in 1951–52. Her designation changed to R71 under the NATO designation system. Refitted in the early 1950s and loaned to Australia on 13 November 1952 as HMAS *Vengeance*, she was sold to Brazil on 12 December 1956. Refitted at Rotterdam between 1957 and 1960, she was recommissioned on 6 December 1960 as the *Minas Gerais* (A11). Refitted in 1976–80, she was laid up in 1987 due to catapult problems. She was refitted again between 1991 and 1993, her catapult becoming operational in 1996. During the 1990s she operated only anti-submarine warfare (ASW) helicopters, but A-4 Skyhawk aircraft have since been acquired. Her armament includes Mistral surface-to-air missiles (SAMs) and 40mm and 47mm guns.

SPECIFICATIONS

Type:	*light aircraft carrier*
Crew:	*1300*
Displacement:	*20,208 tonnes (19,890 tons)*
Length:	*211.8m (694.88ft)*
Beam:	*24.4m (80ft)*
Draught:	*7.5m (24.6ft)*
Speed:	*24 knots*
Range:	*19,308km (12,000 miles)*
Missiles:	*Mistral SAM*
Guns:	*10 x 40mm, 2 x 47mm*
Torpedoes:	*none*
Helicopters:	*6 x H-3, 2 x UH-1, 3 x Super Puma*
Aircraft:	*6 x S-2G Trackers*
Air Search Radar:	*SPS 40B*
Surface Radar:	*Plessey AWS 4*
Fire Control Radar:	*2 x SPG 34*
Propulsion:	*steam turbines, 40,000shp*

HALIFAX

Incorporating many technological advances, including an integrated communications system, a command and control system, and a machinery control system, the Halifax class multirole frigates' weapons, sensors and engines form a significant platform of defensive and offensive capabilities. These ships are quiet, fast and have excellent sea-keeping characteristics. Halifax class frigates deploy singly or as part of a task group anywhere in the world with NATO ships, US carrier battle groups or in cooperation with other allied vessels. These deployments would not be possible without a fleet of modern, versatile patrol frigates. The frigates carry a formidable array of weapons and sensor systems including eight Harpoon long-range surface-to-surface missiles (SSMs) and also termed anti-ship missiles (ASMs), 16 Sea Sparrow surface-to-air missiles (SAMs), a Bofors 57mm rapid-fire gun, a 20mm Phalanx anti-missile close-in weapons system (CIWS), eight 12.7mm machine guns and 24 anti-submarine homing torpedoes. In addition, the ships can defend themselves using infrared suppression, Shield decoys, chaff, flares, a towed acoustic decoy, and radar and sonar jamming devices. Finally, each ship's torpedo-carrying Sea King helicopter significantly extends its overall range of operational effectiveness.

SPECIFICATIONS

Type:	multirole frigate
Crew:	225
Displacement:	5319 tonnes (5235 tons)
Length:	134.7m (441.92ft)
Beam:	16.4m (53.8ft)
Draught:	4.9m (16ft)
Speed:	28 knots
Range:	11,424km (7100 miles)
Missiles:	Harpoon ASM, Sea Sparrow SAM
Guns:	1 x 57mm, 1 x Phalanx
Torpedoes:	Mk 32
Helicopters:	1 x Sea King
Aircraft:	none
Air Search Radar:	SPS 49 (V) 5
Surface Radar:	Ericsson Sea Giraffe HC 150
Fire Control Radar:	2 x Signaal VM 25 STIR
Propulsion:	1 x diesel, 2 x turbines, 47,494shp

IROQUOIS

After years as a pre-eminent anti-submarine warfare vessel during the latter stages of the Cold War, *Iroquois* and her three sisters – *Huron*, *Athabaskan* and *Algonquin* – were refitted in the early 1990s as "command and control ships" with upgraded anti-aircraft defences and improved communications and sensor systems. *Iroquois* and *Algonquin* were further upgraded in the late 1990s. In the aftermath of the 1982 Falklands War (where British warships were sunk by bombs dropped from aircraft and seaskimming missiles) and the war in the Persian Gulf in 1991 where the Allied coalition fleet came under attack from Chinese-made Silkworm surface-to-surface missiles (SSMs), addressing the problem of air defence became a top priority for Western navies. The Canadian Navy decided to convert the four 280s to the area air defence role. This gave them the self-defensive capabilities they needed to become command and control ships. Thus equipped, the navy could form independent task groups, responsible for their own security. As well as substantial changes to the superstructure of the vessels, new air defence weapons were installed including standard vertically launched missiles and a 76mm Super Rapid gun. The Phalanx close-in weapons system (CIWS) provides a final defence against sea-skimming missiles.

SPECIFICATIONS

Type:	air defence destroyer
Crew:	280
Displacement:	5020 tonnes (5100 tonnes)
Length:	129.8m (425.85ft)
Beam:	15.2m (49.86ft)
Draught:	4.7m (15.41ft)
Speed:	29 knots
Range:	7240km (4500 miles)
Missiles:	Mk 41 SAM
Guns:	1 x 76mm, 1 x 20mm, 1 x Phalanx
Torpedoes:	Mk 46
Helicopters:	2 x Sea King
Aircraft:	none
Air Search Radar:	Signaal LW 08
Surface Radar:	Signaal DA 08
Fire Control Radar:	Signaal STIR 1 8
Propulsion:	2 x gas turbines, 50,000shp

LUDA

The Chinese Type 051 Luda class guided missile destroyers are similar to the discontinued Soviet Kotlin class. Intended for anti-ship missions, their primary offensive armament is a pair of "Sea Eagle I" ship-to-ship missiles (SSMs). However, the combat potential provided by the high speed and long range of this ship design was compromised by the lack of an air defence ability. In common with the old Soviet Kotlin class, the Luda class ships originally had no surface-to-air missiles (SAMs) for self-protection, a deficiency which the Soviet Navy eventually remedied with the SAM Kotlin class. Three major Luda variants have been produced: Luda I had an initial basic configuration, though with considerable variations in armament and electronics among its various units; the Luda II added the eight-cell HQ-7 SAM system, along with a helicopter deck and hangar replacing the aft gun armament; and the Luda III features improved sonars, SSMs and electronics on a single ship, the DD166 Zhuhai. The initial Luda I design has now been extensively modernized, primarily for anti-submarine warfare missions, becoming Luda III class. However, thus far only one vessel has been identified (hull number 166, possibly changed to 168 for overseas deployment), but more Luda Is are expected to be upgraded to the Luda III standard in the future.

SPECIFICATIONS

Type:	guided missile destroyer
Crew:	280
Displacement:	3729 tonnes (3670 tons)
Length:	132m (433ft)
Beam:	12.8m (41.99ft)
Draught:	4.6m (15.09ft)
Speed:	32 knots
Range:	4779km (2970 miles)
Missiles:	Sea Eagle SSM, Crotale SAM
Guns:	4 x 130mm, 8 x 57, 37 & 25mm
Torpedoes:	Whitehead A 244S
Helicopters:	2 x Harbin Z-9A
Aircraft:	none
Air Search Radar:	Knife Rest or Cross Slot
Surface Radar:	Eye Shield or Sea Tiger
Fire Control Radar:	Wasp Head or Type 343 Sun Visor B
Propulsion:	steam turbines, 60,000shp

CASSARD

The French Navy's Cassard class destroyer is equipped with the Senit combat data system and an OPSMER command support system. Senit gathers, correlates, evaluates and displays information from shipboard sensors and handles data exchanges with other units, via tactical data links, including Link 11 and 14 and the Syracuse satellite communications system. Two four-cell missile launchers for the Exocet MM40 anti-ship missile (ASM) are installed in a midship position between the two citadels. Two Sadral six-round turrets for the Mistral surface-to-air missile (SAM) are mounted on the raised deck each side of the helicopter hangar. The infrared-guided Mistral provides short-range air defence up to a range of 5km (3.1 miles). The main gun is the DCN 100mm model, which is capable of firing at a rate of 80 rounds per minute up to a range of 8km (5 miles). The ship also has two Oerlikon 20mm guns, which have a range of 10km (6.25 miles) and a firing rate of 720 rounds per minute. The ship has a flight deck at the stern with a single landing spot for the AS 565MA Panther helicopter. To facilitate all-weather operations, the DCN Samahe helicopter handling system allows deployment and recovery of the aircraft in rough seas. In addition, the ship stores an arsenal of helicopter-launched Mark 46 torpedoes.

SPECIFICATIONS

Type:	destroyer
Crew:	245
Displacement:	4775 tonnes (4700 tons)
Length:	139m (456ft)
Beam:	14m (45.93ft)
Draught:	6.5m (21.32ft)
Speed:	29.5 knots
Range:	13,194km (8200 miles)
Missiles:	Exocet ASM, Mistral SAM
Guns:	1 x 100mm, 2 x 20mm
Torpedoes:	KD 59E, ECAN L5 Mod 4
Helicopters:	1 x AS 565MA Panther
Aircraft:	none
Air Search Radar:	DRBJ 11 B, 3D
Surface Radar:	DRBV 26C
Fire Control Radar:	DRBC 33A
Propulsion:	4 x diesels, 43,200shp

CASSIOPÉE

French mine warfare units are tasked with permanently securing the approaches to the Brest Ship, Submersible, Ballistic, Nuclear (SSBN) base, one of France's strategic ports. In the event of particular threats they must also be in a position to simultaneously keep open the ports on the Channel–Atlantic seaboard, in Toulon and Marseilles-Fos, and to keep forces on standby to ensure free access to any and all allied ports. They also constitute a major component for operations involving projection of forces inshore, which are more sensitive to the mine threat. In order to fulfil these missions, the Naval Action Force includes minehunters fitted with the equipment required to identify and destroy devices laid on the sea bed, teams of clearance divers who operate in shallow waters, and sonar tugs to guard the approaches to Brest itself. The *Cassiopée* is one of the Eridan class of minehunters, which have a minimal light minesweeping capability. In January 2000, Directions des Constructions Navales and Thomson Marconi Sonar SAS were awarded parallel contracts to update all 13 of the French Navy's Eridan class "Tripartite" minehunters with a propelled variable depth sonar (PVDS) capability, a new hull-mounted minehunting sonar and a new mine warfare tactical system.

SPECIFICATIONS

Type:	*minehunter*
Crew:	*49*
Displacement:	*605 tonnes (595 tons)*
Length:	*51.6m (169.29ft)*
Beam:	*9m (29.52ft)*
Draught:	*3.5m (11.48ft)*
Speed:	*15 knots*
Range:	*4827km (3000 miles)*
Missiles:	*none*
Guns:	*1 x 20mm, 2 x 12.7mm*
Torpedoes:	*none*
Helicopters:	*none*
Aircraft:	*none*
Air Search Radar:	*none*
Surface Radar:	*Decca 1229*
Fire Control Radar:	*none*
Propulsion:	*1 x diesel, 1900shp*

CHARLES DE GAULLE

The nuclear-powered aircraft carrier *Charles De Gaulle* was constructed at the Brest Naval Shipyard in Brittany. The ship was launched in May 1994 and commissioned in September 2000, following sea trials which began in January 1999. The ship operates a fleet of 40 aircraft: Rafale M, Super Etendard and three E-2C Hawkeye airborne early warning (AEW) aircraft. The ship will also support the AS 565 Panther or NH 90 helicopter. The main deck consists of a main runway angled at 8.5 degrees to the ship's axis and an aircraft launch area forward of the island. These are each equipped with a US Navy Type C13 catapult, capable of launching one aircraft per minute. The carrier is fitted with the SATRAP computerized, integrated stabilization system designed to maintain stabilization to within 0.5 degrees of horizontal, allowing aircraft to operate in rough seas. The Aster 15 surface-to-air missile (SAM) provides defence against hostile aircraft and anti-ship missiles. Two eight-cell Sylver vertical launch systems are installed on the starboard side forward of the bridge and two on the port side aft of the bridge. The ship has two six-cell Sadral launching systems for the Mistral SAM. The nuclear propulsion system has the capacity to provide five years of continuous operation at 25 knots before refuelling.

SPECIFICATIONS

Type:	aircraft carrier
Crew:	1950 (including air wing)
Displacement:	38,000 tonnes (37,401 tons)
Length:	216.5m (710.3ft)
Beam:	31.5m (103.34ft)
Draught:	8.45m (27.72ft)
Speed:	25 knots
Range:	unlimited
Missiles:	Aster 15 SAM, Mistral SAM
Guns:	8 x 20mm
Torpedoes:	none
Helicopters:	see below
Aircraft:	40 (including helicopters)
Air Search Radar:	DRBV 15 3-D, DRBJ 11B
Surface Radar:	DRBV 15C Sea Tiger Mark 2
Fire Control Radar:	Arabel missile control
Propulsion:	nuclear, 83,000shp

FLOREAL

The *Floreal* is the lead ship of a class of French Navy low-cost patrol vessels for overseas service and fisheries patrol. Officially described as surveillance ships designed to operate offshore in low-intensity operations, they have been built to civilian commercial standards, yet appear to provide adequate military features such as survivability (it is important to remember that the manufacturing regulations for the construction of dangerous cargo ships and the quality required for passenger liners are very strict and exhaustive; indeed, they are very similar to those required of naval ships). The vessels of this class feature the modular construction of systems and subsystems throughout, and particularly in the main and auxiliary machinery spaces. Once put together the modules are well arranged and compact, yet items are accessible at all times. Passage around each module on the boat for crew members is easy and does not require manoeuvring around protruding objects. As well as the crew of 80 sailors and officers, the ship has room to accommodate up to 24 special forces personnel. The aft helicopter deck and hangar is for the use and storage of one Panther helicopter. There are six vessels in this class: F730 *Floreal*, F731 *Prairial*, F732 *Nivose*, F733 *Ventose*, F734 *Vendermaire* and F735 *Germinal* (shown above).

SPECIFICATIONS

Type:	*patrol frigate*
Crew:	*80*
Displacement:	*2997 tonnes (2950 tons)*
Length:	*93.5m (306.75ft)*
Beam:	*14m (45.93ft)*
Draught:	*4.3m (14.1ft)*
Speed:	*20 knots*
Range:	*16,090km (10,000 miles)*
Missiles:	*Exocet SSM*
Guns:	*1 x 100mm, 2 x 20mm*
Torpedoes:	*none*
Helicopters:	*1 x Panther*
Aircraft:	*none*
Air Search Radar:	*DRBV 21A*
Surface Radar:	*DRBV 21A*
Fire Control Radar:	*none*
Propulsion:	*4 x diesels, 8800shp*

FOCH

The carriers of the Clemenceau class have been France's premier naval ships since World War II. The *Clemenceau* was decommissioned in October 1997 and the *Foch* will either be held in reserve as a back-up for the new *Charles De Gaulle* nuclear carrier (see page 13) or transferred to the Brazilian Navy for further service there. The ship's air wing includes the Super Etendard, which is configured to carry the ASMP (*Air-Sol Moyenne Portée*) nuclear missile, which is powered by a ramjet with an integrated accelerator. Armed with a tactical nuclear warhead, the ASMP is produced by Aerospatiale, except for the military head, which is provided by the Atomic Energy Commission. The ASMP's nuclear warhead has five times the power of the freefall weapons it replaces. This supersonic missile is guided by a stand-alone system of inertial navigation that provides it with the precision required and allows the launcher aircraft to remain a safe distance from the enemy defences (which is a bonus for the slow-moving Super Etendard). The missile's propulsion system consists of a statoréacteur using liquid fuel developed by Aerospatiale. ASMP became operational in May 1986 on Mirage IVP aircraft and beginning in 1988 on Mirage 2000N aircraft; and it is also being adapted on Super Etendard aircraft for the French Navy.

SPECIFICATIONS

Type:	aircraft carrier
Crew:	1338 plus 582 air wing
Displacement:	33,304 tonnes (32,780 tons)
Length:	265m (869.42ft)
Beam:	31.7m (104ft)
Draught:	8.6m (28.21ft)
Speed:	32 knots
Range:	12,067km (7500 miles)
Missiles:	Crotale SAM
Guns:	4 x 100mm
Torpedoes:	none
Helicopters:	4 (40 for amphibious assault)
Aircraft:	35
Air Search Radar:	DRBV 23B
Surface Radar:	DRBI 10, 1 DRBV 15
Fire Control Radar:	2 x DRBC 32B
Propulsion:	steam turbines, 126,000shp

FOUDRE

The French Navy operates two Foudre class landing platform dock ships, the *Foudre* (L9011) and the *Siroco* (L9012), which were commissioned in 1990 and 1998 respectively. They were built at the Brest Naval Dockyard. The ships are assigned to the Naval Action Force based at the Toulon Mediterranean Command. The Foudre class is capable of landing and supporting a mechanized armoured regiment of the French rapid deployment force. The three main missions of the Foudre class are the landing of infantry and armoured vehicles on unprepared coasts, mobile logistic support for naval forces, and humanitarian missions. The ship's complement is 210 crew with 13 officers; it can also accommodate 467 passengers or troops. With 700 crew and passengers, the ship has an endurance of 30 days. In times of crisis the ship can accommodate up to 1600 people. To meet military and humanitarian requirements, Foudre class ships provide hospital facilities for large-scale medical and evacuation missions, including two fully equipped operating theatres and 47 beds. The ship can accommodate up to seven Super Puma helicopters and the flight deck is equipped with a Samahe haul-down system. The helicopter hangar has capacity for two Super Frelon helicopters or up to four Super Puma helicopters.

SPECIFICATIONS

Type:	*landing platform dock*
Crew:	*223*
Displacement:	*12,090 tonnes (11,900 tons)*
Length:	*168m (551.18ft)*
Beam:	*23.5m (77ft)*
Draught:	*5.2m (17ft)*
Speed:	*21 knots*
Range:	*17,699km (11,000 miles)*
Missiles:	*Simbad SAM*
Guns:	*1 x 40mm, 2 x 20mm*
Torpedoes:	*none*
Helicopters:	*7 x Super Puma*
Aircraft:	*none*
Air Search Radar:	*DRBV 21A*
Surface Radar:	*Racal Decca 2459*
Fire Control Radar:	*none*
Propulsion:	*2 x diesels, 21,600shp*

GEORGES LEYGUES

The Georges Leygues class frigates are assigned the general roles of protection and defence of French and European maritime interests in coordination with allies; ensuring the military presence of France all over the world and the protection of French citizens worldwide; public service missions such as surveillance and rescuing of people and property; and general humanitarian operations. Designed mainly to maintain and enforce French interests in overseas maritime areas and to participate in crisis management outside Europe, these warships are also integrated into the French Carrier Group formation when required. They may thus be used, as part of these missions, to provide support for an intervention force, protection for commercial traffic, or to carry out special operations. The importance attached to reducing their radar and acoustic signatures during construction, their modular design and their high degree of automation make them true twenty-first century ships, innovative in more ways than one. At sea their equipment and weapons are more specifically suited to fighting conventional submarines, especially in shallow waters. The increasing number of submarines deployed by secondary navies throughout the world, plus the increase in amphibious operations, make these warships highly important to the French Navy.

SPECIFICATIONS

Type:	frigate
Crew:	235
Displacement:	4420 tonnes (4350 tons)
Length:	139m (456ft)
Beam:	14m (45.93ft)
Draught:	5.7m (18.7ft)
Speed:	30 knots
Range:	13,676km (8500 miles)
Missiles:	Exocet SSM, Crotale SAM
Guns:	1 x 100mm, 2 x 20mm
Torpedoes:	Mk 46
Helicopters:	2 x Sea Lynx
Aircraft:	none
Air Search Radar:	DRBV 26
Surface Radar:	DRBV 51C
Fire Control Radar:	Thomson-CSF Vega with DRBC 32E
Propulsion:	2 x diesels, 52,000shp

JEANNE D'ARC

A combination of helicopter ship and cruiser, *Jeanne d'Arc* is a training ship in peacetime and an anti-submarine warfare (ASW) or assault ship in wartime. Originally intended only for training to replace a prewar cruiser, she was redesigned with ASW and assault capabilities due to a general shuffling of duties among the French carriers. *Jeanne d'Arc* has a large helicopter deck aft with a hangar below, and a midship superstructure with cruiser-type weapons mounted forward. She is lightly armed, reflecting her training role. During construction the gun armament was reduced, and an ASW rocket launcher eliminated. The hangar is used for berthing and other functions in peacetime but can be quickly reconverted for aircraft if needed. In 1975 six Exocet surface-to-surface missiles (SSMs) were fitted. Exocet missiles started development in 1967, originally as the ship-launched variant MM 38 which entered service in 1975. The air-launched version, AM 39, was developed later starting in 1974 and entering service with the French Navy in 1979. The missile is designed to attack large warships. A block 2 upgrade programme was carried out from the late 1980s until 1993, which introduced an improved digital active radar seeker and upgraded inertial navigation and control electronics.

SPECIFICATIONS

Type:	*helicopter carrier*
Crew:	*696 plus 140 cadets*
Displacement:	*13,482 tonnes (13,270 tons)*
Length:	*182m (597.11ft)*
Beam:	*24m (78.74ft)*
Draught:	*7.3m (23.95ft)*
Speed:	*26 knots*
Range:	*9654km (6000 miles)*
Missiles:	*Exocet SSM*
Guns:	*4 x 100mm*
Torpedoes:	*none*
Helicopters:	*4 x Alouette, 8 x Super Puma*
Aircraft:	*none*
Air Search Radar:	*DRBV 22D*
Surface Radar:	*DRBV 51*
Fire Control Radar:	*3 x DRBC 32A*
Propulsion:	*1 x steam turbine, 40,000shp*

LA MOTTE-PICQUET

This Georges Leygues class frigate is named after the French Admiral Toussaint Guillaume Picquet De La Motte (1720–91), who fought the English in the Caribbean during the American Revolutionary War. He was victorious in several key engagements and made an important visit to Savannah, Georgia, in 1779 in support of American independence. FS *La Motte-Picquet* (D645), commissioned in 1988, is a frigate specializing in anti-submarine warfare. The ship carries up to 26 Crotale surface-to-air missiles (SAMs). The Crotale system provides air situation and threat assessment, extended detection range, Identification Friend-or-Foe (IFF), multi-target detection plus automated acquisition, tracking and engagement and all-weather operation. The Crotale NG VT1 missile features a high level of manoeuvrability: speed is Mach 3.5, using a solid propellant rocket motor. The VT1 has an effective range of about 11km (6.87 miles) and ceiling of over 6000m (19,685ft). The command to line-of-sight (CLOS) guidance uses radar and electro-optical sensors. The missile is armed with a focused blast and fragmentation warhead, initiated by a proximity fuse. The warhead provides a lethal blast radius of 8m (26.24ft). Typical interception time from firing to airborne target destruction at a distance of 8km (5 miles) is 10.3 seconds.

SPECIFICATIONS

Type:	frigate
Crew:	235
Displacement:	4420 tonnes (4350 tons)
Length:	139m (456ft)
Beam:	14m (45.93ft)
Draught:	5.7m (18.7ft)
Speed:	30 knots
Range:	13,676km (8500 miles)
Missiles:	Exocet SSM, Crotale SAM
Guns:	1 x 100mm, 2 x 20mm
Torpedoes:	Mk 46
Helicopters:	2 x Lynx
Aircraft:	none
Air Search Radar:	DRBV 26
Surface Radar:	DRBV 51C
Fire Control Radar:	DRBC 32E
Propulsion:	2 x diesels, 52,000shp

L'AUDACIEUSE

The L'audacieuse class of offshore patrol boats is designed for overseas service. The main armament is a 40mm gun – an all-round weapon system with high development potential, and a gun that can be used with equal lethality in the traditional roles of field air defence or for combating ground threats. The gun fires a Bofors 3P round, which is state-of-the-art in terms of proximity fuzed ammunition: a multi-role round so versatile that it can be used against all targets within the aerial threat concept – aircraft, helicopters and stand-off weapons – as well as ground targets with the same lethal effect. The 3P round has an increased tungsten pellet payload and is the heaviest, most powerful shell in the 40mm family of ammunition. Its programmable fuze optimizes the effect against the target and increases the tactical flexibility of the 40mm weapon system by communication with the fire control system via a proximity fuze programmer. The 12.7mm machine gun (M2HB-QCB), of which the ship has two, is capable of firing explosive incendiary rounds and a full range of ball, tracer, armour-piercing and incendiary cartridges. In service around the world, it is the ideal weapon to mount on soft-skinned and armoured vehicles and also on patrol boats as the main or secondary armament.

SPECIFICATIONS

Type:	offshore patrol boat
Crew:	24
Displacement:	461 tonnes (454 tons)
Length:	54.5m (178.8ft)
Beam:	8m (26.24ft)
Draught:	2.5m (8.2ft)
Speed:	24.5 knots
Range:	6758km (4200 miles)
Missiles:	none
Guns:	1 x 40mm, 1 x 20mm, 2 x 12.7mm
Torpedoes:	none
Helicopters:	none
Aircraft:	none
Air Search Radar:	none
Surface Radar:	Decca 1226
Fire Control Radar:	none
Propulsion:	2 x diesels, 8000shp

SUFFREN

The Suffren class was the first French destroyer designed from the outset to carry surface-to-air missiles (SAMs). Three ships were planned with more to follow, but budget cutbacks reduced this number down to two. They have been significantly modernized over the years and will serve well into the twenty-first century. They are primarily used as air defence ships for French carriers. Anti-aircraft destroyers in general are intended to provide protection for maritime forces against missiles and air threats. They contribute to the surveillance and control of air space and have the task of intervening in any zone within a group, according to the needs of the mission. In air engagements, initial target detection is usually provided by the long-range air search radar. This is a three-dimensional, electronically stabilized, computer-controlled radar, which includes an automatic detection and tracking (ADT) capability. Target data is transferred, automatically or manually, to the computer of the Naval Tactical Data System (NTDS). NTDS forms the heart of the combat system, tying together the various subsystems, which collects and processes information from ship sensors, and from off-ship sensors, via radio digital data links. From NTDS, air targets are then sent to the weapons for actual engagement.

SPECIFICATIONS

Type:	destroyer
Crew:	355
Displacement:	7020 tonnes (6910 tons)
Length:	157.6m (517ft)
Beam:	15.5m (50.85ft)
Draught:	6.1m (20ft)
Speed:	34 knots
Range:	8206km (5100 miles)
Missiles:	Exocet, Masurca, Malafon
Guns:	2 x 100mm, 4–6 x 20mm
Torpedoes:	none
Helicopters:	none
Aircraft:	none
Air Search Radar:	DRBI 23
Surface Radar:	DRBV 1 SA
Fire Control Radar:	2 x DRBR 51, 1 x DRBC 33A
Propulsion:	steam turbines, 72,500shp

BRANDENBURG

The Type 123 Brandenburg class frigates were ordered in June 1989 to replace the Hamburg class. The frigates are primarily tasked with anti-submarine operations, but also contribute to anti-air defence, the tactical command of group forces and surface operations. The ships form part of the Wilhelmshaven-based 6th Frigate Squadron. They are armed with two twin launchers for Exocet surface-to-surface missiles (SSMs). A Lockheed Martin Mk 41 Mod 3 vertical launch system for 16 NATO Sea Sparrow medium-range SAMs is fitted. The ships also have two 21-cell launchers for the RAM (Rolling Airframe) short-range SAM. The RAM missile has infrared guidance and a range of 9.5km (15.28 miles). The ships' main gun is the Otobreda 76mm/62 Mk 75, which has a firing rate of 85 rounds per minute and a range of 16km (25.74 miles) anti-surface and 12km (19.3 miles) anti-air. There are also two 20mm Rh 202 guns. Two twin 324mm Mk 32 torpedo tubes are fitted for the AlliantTechsystems Mk 46 active/-passive anti-submarine torpedo. The electronic warfare suite includes the FL 1800 S-II electronic support measures and countermeasures system, developed by Daimler Chrysler Aerospace. In addition, two Otobreda SCLAR decoy dispensers are fitted for chaff and infrared flares.

SPECIFICATIONS

Type:	frigate
Crew:	218
Displacement:	4775 tonnes (4700 tons)
Length:	138.9m (455.7ft)
Beam:	16.7m (54.79ft)
Draught:	6.3m (20.66ft)
Speed:	29 knots
Range:	6436km (4000 miles)
Missiles:	Exocet SSM, Sea Sparrow, RAM
Guns:	1 x 76mm, 2 x 20mm
Torpedoes:	Mk 32, Mk 46
Helicopters:	2 x Sea Lynx
Aircraft:	none
Air Search Radar:	Signaal LW 08
Surface Radar:	Signaal SMART, 3D
Fire Control Radar:	2 x Signaal STIR 180 trackers
Propulsion:	2 x gas turbines, 51,680shp

BREMEN

The *Bremen* is designed primarily for anti-surface warfare missions with strong anti-air and anti-submarine warfare capability. Her combat system integrates target acquisition, navigation, communications, signal processing and weapon control functions, and the combat system's central computer calculates and evaluates the target data and then allocates data to the weapon systems. The system carries out multiple target search and track, target prioritization and automatic engagement of weapons. The ship's point defence system is based on the medium-range Sea Sparrow and the short-range RAM (Rolling Airframe) missile. Sea Sparrow is launched from two Mk 29 eight-cell launchers mounted side by side at the fore of the ship, above and behind the Otobreda gun. The RAM (RIM-116A) is installed at the aft of the ship above the helicopter deck. The ship is equipped with a 76mm Otobreda anti-air and anti-surface gun, and two 20mm guns are installed port and starboard. The ship accommodates two Sea Lynx helicopters, which are equipped with AQS-18D dipping sonar and two torpedoes: either Mk 46 or DM4 type. The hangar provides space, facilities and equipment for the maintenance of the two helicopters, and the flight deck is large enough for landing a Sea King-type helicopter.

SPECIFICATIONS

Type:	*frigate*
Crew:	*200*
Displacement:	*3658 tonnes (3600 tons)*
Length:	*130m (426.5ft)*
Beam:	*14.5m (47.57ft)*
Draught:	*4.26m (13.97ft)*
Speed:	*30 knots*
Range:	*6436km (4000 miles)*
Missiles:	*Harpoon, Sea Sparrow, RAM*
Guns:	*1 x 76mm, 2 x 20mm*
Torpedoes:	*Mk 32, Mk 46*
Helicopters:	*2 x Sea Lynx*
Aircraft:	*none*
Air Search Radar:	*Signaal DA 08*
Surface Radar:	*Signaal DA 08*
Fire Control Radar:	*Signaal WM 25, Signaal STIR*
Propulsion:	*2 x gas turbines, 50,000shp*

LUTJENS

The *Lutjens* is one of the two American Charles F. Adams class guided missile destroyers constructed in the late 1950s and early 1960s which Germany purchased. Despite periodic modernizations, the class was retired in the early 1990s from the US Navy. Modernization with the New Threat Upgrade (NTU) package was considered for these ships but was terminated since modernization would not have been cost effective given their limited service lives remaining. They have suffered severe machinery problems and are overdue for replacement. Notwithstanding mechanical problems, their armament is good. For example, they are equipped with Harpoon surface-to-surface missiles (SSMs). Their low-level, sea-skimming cruise trajectory, active radar guidance and warhead design assure high survivability and effectiveness. The Harpoon missile and its launch control equipment provide the capability to interdict ships at ranges well beyond those of other missiles. Once targeting information is obtained and sent to the Harpoon missile, it is fired. Once fired, the missile flies to the target location, turns on its seeker, locates the target and strikes it without further action from the firing platform. This allows the firing platform to engage other threats instead of concentrating on one at a time.

SPECIFICATIONS

Type:	destroyer
Crew:	340
Displacement:	4572 tonnes (4500 tons)
Length:	133.2m (437ft)
Beam:	14.3m (46.91ft)
Draught:	4.5m (14.76ft)
Speed:	32 knots
Range:	7200km (4500 miles)
Missiles:	Harpoon SSM, RAM
Guns:	2 x 20mm
Torpedoes:	Mk 46
Helicopters:	none
Aircraft:	none
Air Search Radar:	Lockheed SPS 40, Hughes SPS 52
Surface Radar:	Raytheon/Sylvania SPS 10
Fire Control Radar:	2 x Raytheon SPG 51, SPQ 9
Propulsion:	2 x steam turbines, 70,000shp

HMS CAMPBELTOWN

The *Campbeltown* is one of the four Type 22 Batch 3 frigates in Royal Navy service. The Type 22 is significantly larger than its more recent cousin, the Type 23. A major difference is that the Type 22 can accommodate two Lynx helicopters whereas the Type 23 can only accommodate one. However, in times of peace it is usual for only one Lynx to be deployed. Given that the Lynx is a powerful anti-submarine aircraft, this gives the Type 22 a more powerful offensive role. On the negative side, however, is the fact that in both the Batch 2 and Batch 3 frigates, the Sea Wolf SAM system is mounted in launchers which means that the ship does not have 360-degree defence from air attacks. The Type 22 frigate is now relatively old but it has served the Royal Navy well, and it is likely that when the next three Type 23 frigates enter service, the remaining three Batch 2 frigates will be paid off. What replaces the Batch 3 ships is yet to be decided, but that batch still has some operational life left. The Batch 3 remains a very versatile ship. Its offensive weaponry is a match to the Type 23, and its extra helicopter capability is an advantage. However, the Type 22 does not have the same stealth characteristics of the Type 23 and so it is likely that the Type 22 will be of more use in an escort role rather than as an independent command.

SPECIFICATIONS

Type:	frigate
Crew:	259
Displacement:	4978 tonnes (4900 tons)
Length:	148.1m (485.89ft)
Beam:	14.8m (48.55ft)
Draught:	6.4m (20.99ft)
Speed:	30 knots
Range:	7200km (4500 miles)
Missiles:	Harpoon SSM, Sea Wolf SAM
Guns:	1 x 4.5in, 1 x Goalkeeper, 2 x 30mm
Torpedoes:	Marconi Stingray
Helicopters:	2 x Sea Lynx or EH101 Merlin
Aircraft:	none
Air Search Radar:	Marconi Type 967/968
Surface Radar:	Marconi Type 967/968
Fire Control Radar:	2 x Marconi Type 911
Propulsion:	2 x gas turbines, 37,540shp

HMS CATTISTOCK

The Hunt class was envisaged as a sophisticated minesweeper designed principally to work in coastal and shallow water areas, such as the approaches to the River Clyde, where many of Britain's nuclear submarines are based. The ships were designed with noise-reduction features to avoid accidentally triggering mines. The Hunt class combines the roles of minehunter and minesweeper. There are three ways the ships can neutralize mines: towing wire sweeps in order to severe moored mines, so they rise to the surface and can then be destroyed by gunfire; using acoustic or influence sweeps to trigger mines on the seabed; and identifying mines on the sonar and then using clearance divers to place charges on them. The Hunt class also carries the Remote Control Mine Disposal System (RCMDS). This is a small, unmanned, remote-controlled submarine that can destroy underwater mines using explosives. Although the Hunt class ships have been criticized for being costly and for performing poorly in rough weather, when they entered service they were the most advanced mine warfare vessels on the naval scene and the world's largest Glass Reinforced Plastic (GRP) warships. These vessels have also served in the waters off Northern Ireland, where they have undertaken counter-terrorist missions close inshore.

SPECIFICATIONS

Type:	mine countermeasures vessel
Crew:	45
Displacement:	737 tonnes (725 tons)
Length:	60m (196.85ft)
Beam:	9.85m (32.31ft)
Draught:	2.2m (7.21ft)
Speed:	14 knots
Range:	4800km (3000 miles)
Missiles:	none
Guns:	1 x 30mm, 2 x 7.62mm
Torpedoes:	none
Helicopters:	none
Aircraft:	none
Air Search Radar:	none
Surface Radar:	Type 1007 I band
Fire Control Radar:	none
Propulsion:	2 x diesels

HMS CORNWALL

HMS *Cornwall* is the lead vessel of the new Eight Frigate Squadron consisting of her sister ships HMS *Cumberland*, *Campbeltown* and *Chatham*. She was launched on 14 October 1985 and commissioned in Falmouth, Cornwall, on 23 April 1988. She was the first Type 22 Batch 3 frigate, designed to detect and destroy submarines at long range using bow mounted "active" and towed-array "passive" sonars, plus torpedoes fired from triple tubes or dropped from the ship's helicopter. She is the first British ship to be fitted with Harpoon anti-ship missiles (ASMs), giving her an extensive anti-surface capability. The Sea Wolf and Goalkeeper anti-missile systems give the ship excellent self-defence against all airborne targets, including sea-skimming missiles. There are two main differences between the Batch 2 and Batch 3 Type 22s. The first is that the Batch 3 has a 114mm (4.5in) gun. This was a direct consequence of experience in the Falklands War, where it was discovered that the earlier Batch 1 Type 22s were at a disadvantage because of the absence of a gun. The 114mm gun is the same as that found on the Type 23, and is capable of firing at a rate of 25 rounds per minute up to a range of 22km (13.75 miles). The second significant difference is that the Batch 3 is equipped with Harpoon rather than Exocet.

SPECIFICATIONS

Type:	frigate
Crew:	259
Displacement:	4978 tonnes (4900 tons)
Length:	148.1m (485.89ft)
Beam:	14.8m (48.55ft)
Draught:	6.4m (20.99ft)
Speed:	30 knots
Range:	7200km (4500 miles)
Missiles:	Harpoon SSM, Sea Wolf SAM
Guns:	1 x 4.5in, 1 x Goalkeeper, 2 x 30mm
Torpedoes:	Marconi Stingray
Helicopters:	2 x Lynx or EH 101 Merlin
Aircraft:	none
Air Search Radar:	Marconi Type 967/968
Surface Radar:	Marconi Type 967/968
Fire Control Radar:	2 x Marconi Type 911
Propulsion:	2 x gas turbines, 37,540shp

HMS EDINBURGH

HMS *Edinburgh* is one of the youngest of the Type 42 destroyers, having been launched at Cammell Laird, Birkenhead, on 14 April 1983 and commissioned on 17 December 1985. She is a Batch 3 "stretched" Type 42, being some 16m (52.49ft) longer than her older sisters. *Edinburgh* has a crew of 301, including 26 officers. Her completion was delayed by several months to take in modifications as a result of lessons learned in the Falklands War. The Type 42 destroyer is an air defence platform, protecting herself and her group against attacks by enemy aircraft and missiles. She is equipped with Sea Dart surface-to-air missiles (SAMs), a 4.5in gun, Stingray torpedoes and the Vulcan Phalanx system as a last line of defence. Her Lynx helicopter carries Sea Skua anti-ship missiles. She underwent her most recent refit in the mid-1990s, at Rosyth, just across from Edinburgh, and her first deployment was to the Gulf on Armilla patrol. 1997 saw her mainly around the UK coast, with appearances at Staff College Sea Days, Joint Maritime Course, the Perisher (submarine commanders' qualifying course) and visits to Leith and Esbjerg in Denmark. Part of the following year was spent in the South Atlantic, patrolling the Falklands, making numerous visits to South American ports, and exercising with local navies.

SPECIFICATIONS

Type:	*destroyer*
Crew:	*301*
Displacement:	*4750 tonnes (4675 tons)*
Length:	*141.4m (463.91ft)*
Beam:	*14.9m (48.88ft)*
Draught:	*5.8m (19.02ft)*
Speed:	*30 knots*
Range:	*6400km (4000 miles)*
Missiles:	*Sea Dart SAM*
Guns:	*1 x 4.5in, 2 x 20mm, 2 x Phalanx*
Torpedoes:	*Stingray*
Helicopters:	*1 x Lynx*
Aircraft:	*none*
Air Search Radar:	*Marconi/Signaal Type 1022*
Surface Radar:	*Type 996 or Type 992R*
Fire Control Radar:	*2 x Marconi Type 909*
Propulsion:	*2 x gas turbines, 54,400shp*

HMS ILLUSTRIOUS

The Invincible class aircraft carrier HMS *Illustrious* was built at the Swan Hunter Shipbuilders yard in Wallsend and was commissioned in 1982. Her role is to provide a command headquarters for the task group and to support the operations of short take-off and vertical landing aircraft and helicopters. The ship accommodates over 1000 crew, including 350 aircrew with 80 officers. She also has capacity for an additional 500 Royal Marines. HMS *Invincible* and *Illustrious* each have three Thales Nederland Goalkeeper close-in weapons system (CIWS). Goalkeeper's Gatling 30mm gun provides a maximum firing rate of 4200 rounds per minute with a range of 1500m (4921ft). All three carriers are also equipped with two 20mm guns, which have a maximum range of 2km (1.25 miles) and a firing rate of 1000 rounds per minute. The Invincible class is fitted with the Racal Type 675(2) jamming system and either a UAA(2) (*Invincible*, *Ark Royal*) or UAT(8) (*Illustrious*) electronic support measures system also supplied by Racal. *Invincible* and *Ark Royal* are also to be fitted with the UAT ESM. The ship's decoy system is the Royal Navy's Outfit DLJ with Sea Gnat. There are eight 130mm six-barrel launchers produced by Hunting Engineering. Chemring and Pains Wessex produce the Sea Gnat chaff and infrared decoys.

SPECIFICATIONS

Type:	aircraft carrier
Crew:	740 plus 430 aircrew
Displacement:	20,930 tonnes (20,600 tons)
Length:	209.1m (686ft)
Beam:	36m (118.11ft)
Draught:	8m (26.24ft)
Speed:	28 knots
Range:	11,200km (7000 miles)
Missiles:	none
Guns:	3 x Goalkeeper, 2 x 20mm
Torpedoes:	none
Helicopters:	9 x Sea King, 3 x Sea King AEW
Aircraft:	9 x Sea Harrier
Air Search Radar:	Marconi/Signaal Type 1022
Surface Radar:	Marconi Type 992R (R 07)
Fire Control Radar:	2 x Marconi Type 909 or 909(1)
Propulsion:	4 x gas turbines, 94,000shp

HMS INVINCIBLE

The Invincible class aircraft carrier supports nine Harrier aircraft (both the Royal Air Force GR7 Harrier II and the Royal Navy F/A2 Sea Harrier), nine Sea King HAS 6 anti-submarine warfare (ASW) helicopters and three Sea King 2 airborne early warning (AEW) helicopters. Landing trials with the Merlin HM.1 helicopter have taken place on the *Ark Royal*, which will be the first carrier to deploy the Merlin. The helicopter's primary roles are anti-surface ship and submarine warfare, tracking and surveillance, amphibious operations, and search and rescue missions. It will operate from Type 22 and Type 23 class frigates, Invincible class aircraft carriers and various amphibious warfare ships and land bases. The first Merlin entered service with the Royal Navy in December 1998, at Royal Naval Air Station Culdrose, where the first squadron of Merlins was formed in October 2001. In September 2000, Merlin began operational trials on the Type 23 frigate HMS *Lancaster*. The cockpit is equipped with six high-definition colour displays plus an optional pilot's mission display. Dual flight controls are provided for the pilot and co-pilot on all versions of the EH101. The crew of the naval anti-submarine warfare version of the helicopter also includes an observer and an acoustic surveillance systems operator.

SPECIFICATIONS

Type:	aircraft carrier
Crew:	740 plus 430 aircrew
Displacement:	20,930 tonnes (20,600 tons)
Length:	209.1m (686ft)
Beam:	36m (118.11ft)
Draught:	8m (26.24ft)
Speed:	28 knots
Range:	11,200km (7000 miles)
Missiles:	none
Guns:	3 x Goalkeeper, 2 x 20mm
Torpedoes:	none
Helicopters:	9 x Sea King, 3 x Sea King AEW
Aircraft:	9 x Harrier
Air Search Radar:	Marconi/Signaal Type 1022
Surface Radar:	Marconi Type 992R (R 07)
Fire Control Radar:	2 x Marconi Type 909 or 909(1)
Propulsion:	4 x gas turbines, 94,000shp

HMS LIVERPOOL

This Sheffield class guided missile destroyer serves with the 3rd Destroyer Squadron. One of its weapons is the Vulcan Phalanx, which automatically engages functions usually performed by separate, independent systems such as search, detection, threat evaluation, acquisition, track, firing, target destruction, kill assessment and cease fire. Phalanx production started in 1978 with orders for 23 US Navy and 14 Foreign Military Sales (FMS) systems. Phalanx is a point-defence, total-weapon system consisting of two 20mm gun mounts that provide a terminal defence against incoming air targets. This close-in weapons system (CIWS) will automatically engage incoming anti-ship missiles and high-speed, low-level aircraft that have penetrated the ship's primary defence envelope. As a unitized system, CIWS automatically performs search, detecting, tracking, threat evaluation, firing, and kill assessments of targets while providing for manual override. Each gun mount houses a fire control assembly and a gun subsystem. The fire control assembly is composed of a search radar for surveillance and detection of hostile targets and a track radar for aiming the gun while tracking a target. The unique closed-loop fire control system gives CIWS the capability to correct its aim to hit fast-moving targets.

SPECIFICATIONS

Type:	destroyer
Crew:	253
Displacement:	4166 tonnes (4100 tons)
Length:	125m (410.1ft)
Beam:	14.3m (46.91ft)
Draught:	5.8m (19.02ft)
Speed:	29 knots
Range:	6400km (4000 miles)
Missiles:	Sea Dart SAM
Guns:	1 x 4.5in, 2–4 x 20mm, 2 x Phalanx
Torpedoes:	2 x triple torpedo tubes
Helicopters:	1 x Lynx
Aircraft:	none
Air Search Radar:	Marconi/Signaal Type 1022
Surface Radar:	Plessey Type 996
Fire Control Radar:	2 x Marconi Type 909
Propulsion:	2 x gas turbines, 54,000shp

HMS MANCHESTER

The Royal Navy has 11 Type 42 destroyers, also known as the Sheffield and Manchester classes, these being in three batches. HMS *Manchester*, and her sisters HMS *Gloucester*, *Edinburgh* and *York* were completed between 1983 and 1985. The main differences between these Batch 3 ships and the previous Batch 1 and 2 of the class are that the Batch 3 vessels are 16m (52.4ft) longer, slightly faster and have a slightly lower weapons fit, in addition to a slight increase in crew. Scheduled to be replaced by the long-awaited Type 45 destroyers, they will remain in service until at least 2007. The name ship of the class, HMS *Sheffield*, was lost in the Falklands War, as was her sister ship HMS *Coventry*. The original role for the Type 42 destroyer was the area air defence of the carrier/landing fleet, with a secondary anti-submarine role. This role was quite ably filled by the massive Type 82 HMS *Bristol*, but it was clear that this ship was too expensive to be procured in sufficient numbers and to be crewed, and for its size was under armed and had disadvantages, such as lack of a helicopter, a close-range armament system and anti-submarine torpedoes. The Type 42 is a much-reduced "economy" design on the smallest possible hull, with maximum automation for the smallest possible crew, carrying the heaviest possible armament.

SPECIFICATIONS

Type:	destroyer
Crew:	301
Displacement:	4750 tonnes (4675 tons)
Length:	141.4m (463.91ft)
Beam:	14.9m (48.88ft)
Draught:	5.8m (19.02ft)
Speed:	30 knots
Range:	6400km (4000 miles)
Missiles:	Sea Dart SAM
Guns:	1 x 4.5in, 2 x 20mm, 2 x Phalanx
Torpedoes:	Stingray
Helicopters:	1 x Sea Lynx
Aircraft:	none
Air Search Radar:	Marconi/Signaal Type 1022
Surface Radar:	Type 996 or Type 992R
Fire Control Radar:	2 x Marconi Type 909
Propulsion:	2 x gas turbines, 54,400shp

HMS MARLBOROUGH

The Type 23 Duke class was originally designed for anti-submarine warfare (ASW), but the addition of the vertical-launched Sea Wolf point missile defence system and the Harpoon SSM has expanded its role to include anti-surface warfare. Harpoon is undergoing an upgrade programme to improve its capabilities. Harpoon Block II will provide accurate long-range guidance for coastal, littoral and blue water ship targets by incorporating the global positioning system/inertial navigation system (GPS/INS) from the Joint Direct Attack Munitions (JDAM) programme. The existing 227kg (500lb) blast warhead will deliver lethal firepower against targets which include coastal anti-surface missile sites and ships in port. For the anti-ship mission, the GPS/INS provides improved missile guidance to the target area. The accurate navigation solution allows target ship discrimination from a nearby land mass using shoreline data provided by the launch platform. These Block II improvements will maintain Harpoon's high-hit probability while offering a 90 percent improvement in the separation distance between the hostile threat and local shorelines. Harpoon Block II will be capable of deployment from all platforms which currently have the Harpoon missile system by using existing command and launch equipment.

SPECIFICATIONS

Type:	frigate
Crew:	185
Displacement:	4267 tonnes (4200 tons)
Length:	133m (436.35ft)
Beam:	16.1m (52.82ft)
Draught:	5.5m (18.04ft)
Speed:	28 knots
Range:	12,480km (7800 miles)
Missiles:	Harpoon SSM, Sea Wolf SAM
Guns:	1 x 4.5in, 2 x 30mm
Torpedoes:	4 x 324mm tubes
Helicopters:	1 x Sea Lynx or EH101 Merlin
Aircraft:	none
Air Search Radar:	Plessey Type 996 (I), 3D
Surface Radar:	Plessey Type 996 (I), 3D
Fire Control Radar:	2 x Marconi Type 911
Propulsion:	4 x diesels, 52,300shp

HMS MONTROSE

Another of the Type 23 Duke class frigates, *Montrose* is armed with a Vickers 114mm (4.5in) gun that has a range of 22km (13.75 miles) against surface and 6km (3.75 miles) against airborne targets, and two Oerlikon 30mm guns with a range of 10km (6.25 miles) against surface and 3.5km (2.18 miles) against airborne targets. The ship has four 324mm torpedo tubes carrying Stingray torpedoes. Stingray has a depth of 750m (2461ft) and a range of 11km (6.87 miles). The sonar system, which is mounted at the front of the torpedo's guidance and control section, comprises a low-noise array assembly, transmitter unit, receiver and two digital signal processing units. The dual active/passive sonar operates with multiple, selectable transmit and receive beams. The ship's command and control system is a fully distributed Ada system based on technology using Intel processors, INMOS T800 transputers and a dual fibre-optic network. The satellite communications system is the SCOT 1D. Countermeasures systems include four Sea Gnat decoys and a Type 182 towed torpedo decoy. The Sea Gnats are mounted on 130mm six-barrel launchers. Thales Defence UAF-1 ESM is fitted to the first seven ships and Thales Defence's UAT(1) to the rest. The ships also boast the Thales Defence's Scorpion jammer.

SPECIFICATIONS

Type:	frigate
Crew:	185
Displacement:	4267 tonnes (4200 tons)
Length:	133m (436.35ft)
Beam:	16.1m (52.82ft)
Draught:	5.5m (18.04ft)
Speed:	28 knots
Range:	12,480km (7800 miles)
Missiles:	Harpoon SSM, Sea Wolf SAM
Guns:	1 x 4.5in, 2 x 30mm
Torpedoes:	4 x 324mm tubes
Helicopters:	1 x Lynx or EH 101 Merlin
Aircraft:	none
Air Search Radar:	Plessey Type 996 (I), 3D
Surface Radar:	Plessey Type 996 (I), 3D
Fire Control Radar:	2 x Marconi Type 911
Propulsion:	4 x diesels, 52,300shp

HMS NORFOLK

At present the Type 23 frigates have Thomson Marconi Sonar Type 2050 medium-range bow-mounted active/passive search and attack sonar and Thomson Type 2031Z very low-frequency passive search towed array sonar. However, the latter is to be replaced by the Type 2087 low-frequency active sonar (LFAS). This is a variable depth low-frequency transmitter and a passive, towed reception array. A contract for the Type 2087 development has been awarded to Thomson Marconi Sonar. The Type 2087, which is due to enter service in 2006, will have a greater range with bistatic and intercept capability. HMS *Norfolk* has a diesel-electric and gas (CODLAG) system, which consists of two Rolls-Royce Spey SM1A 34000hp gas turbines and two GEC 1.5MW 4400hp electric motors. There are also four GEC-Alsthom Paxman Valenta 12 RP2000CZ 7000hp auxiliary diesels. Using the diesel-electric motors, the economical speed is 15 knots and the range is 12,480km (7800 miles). The Type 23 carries the Lynx ASW helicopter, which is due to be replaced by the EH101 Merlin helicopter which entered service in December 1998. The Merlin helicopter provides search-and-attack capability for ASW and surface surveillance and over-the-horizon targeting for anti-surface warfare.

SPECIFICATIONS

Type:	frigate
Crew:	185
Displacement:	4267 tonnes (4200 tons)
Length:	133m (436.35ft)
Beam:	16.1m (52.82ft)
Draught:	5.5m (18.04ft)
Speed:	28 knots
Range:	12,480km (7800 miles)
Missiles:	Harpoon SSM, Sea Wolf SAM
Guns:	1 x 4.5in, 2 x 30mm
Torpedoes:	4 x 324mm tubes
Helicopters:	1 x Sea Lynx or EH101 Merlin
Aircraft:	none
Air Search Radar:	Plessey Type 996 (I), 3D
Surface Radar:	Plessey Type 996 (I), 3D
Fire Control Radar:	2 x Marconi Type 911
Propulsion:	4 x diesels, 52,300shp

HMS OCEAN

The primary role of HMS *Ocean* is to achieve the rapid landing of an assault force by helicopter and landing craft. The ship carries a crew of 255, an aircrew of 206 and 480 Royal Marines (an extra 320 Royal Marines can be accommodated in a short-term emergency). The ship has capacity for 40 vehicles but is not designed to land heavy tanks. There are four LCVP Mk 5 vehicle/personnel landing craft on davits, and the ship has full facilities for 12 EH101 Merlin and six Lynx helicopters, and landing and refuelling facilities for Chinook helicopters. Twenty Sea Harriers could be carried but not supported. The weapon systems include four Oerlikon twin 30mm guns together with three Phalanx Mk 15 close-in weapon systems (CIWS). HMS *Ocean* is equipped with eight Sea Gnat radar reflection/infrared emitting decoys. Sea Gnat was developed under a NATO collaborative project involving the USA, Germany, Norway, Denmark and Great Britain for protection against anti-ship guided missiles. The electronic support measures system is the Royal Navy's UAT, which is a radar warning receiver and electronic surveillance system that provides targeting data and identification of hostile radar threats. Also fitted is the Thales Type 675(2) shipborne jammer, which has a range of 500km (312 miles).

SPECIFICATIONS

Type:	amphibious helicopter carrier
Crew:	255 + 206 aircrew + 480 Marines
Displacement:	22,108 tonnes (21,760 tons)
Length:	203m (666ft)
Beam:	34m (111.54ft)
Draught:	6.6m (21.65ft)
Speed:	18 knots
Range:	12,800km (8000 miles)
Missiles:	none
Guns:	3 x Phalanx, 4 x twin 30mm
Torpedoes:	none
Helicopters:	12 x EH101 Merlin, 6 x Sea Lynx
Aircraft:	20 x Sea Harrier if no helicopters
Air Search Radar:	Siemens Plessey Type 996
Surface Radar:	2 x Kelvin Hughes Type 1007
Fire Control Radar:	ADAWS 2000 combat data system
Propulsion:	2 x diesels, 47,000shp

HMS SANDOWN

Sandown class minehunters are built almost entirely of non-magnetic materials and are designed to resist high shock levels. Their manoeuvrability is controlled, either manually or automatically, by using the Ship Position Control System (SPCS). The Sandown class is equipped with two underwater PAP 104 Mark 5 Remote Control Mine Disposal Vehicles. The vehicle is controlled via a 2000m (6561ft) fibre-optic cable. A lighting system, low-light level black and white camera and a colour camera are fitted. The vehicle is also fitted with a high-resolution sonar. The sensor data is transmitted back to the operations control centre on the ship. The main payload is a 100kg (220lb) mine-disposal charge which can be replaced by a manipulator. Wire cutters are used to release moored mines from the column of water above the sea bed. The mine disposal vehicles can be deployed to a depth of 300m (984ft). The Batch 2 Sandown class ships have a more powerful crane for deployment and recovery of the remotely controlled vehicles. The ship is equipped with two Barricade lightweight decoy launchers, which are capable of dispensing infrared decoys and chaff in confusion, distraction and centroid seduction modes of operation. The sonar system is the Type 2093 variable depth sonar which is deployed from a well in the hull.

SPECIFICATIONS

Type:	minehunter
Crew:	34
Displacement:	492 tonnes (484 tons)
Length:	52.5m (172.24ft)
Beam:	10.5m (34.44ft)
Draught:	2.3m (7.54ft)
Speed:	13 knots
Range:	4800km (3000 miles)
Missiles:	none
Guns:	1 x 30mm
Torpedoes:	none
Helicopters:	none
Aircraft:	none
Air Search Radar:	none
Surface Radar:	none
Fire Control Radar:	none
Propulsion:	2 x diesels

HMS SCOTT

The hull of the *Scott* survey ship encompasses three equipment/cargo holds, each separated by watertight bulkheads. Additionally, within the hull is a near complete double hull attained through the use of wing, deep and double-bottom tanks throughout her length. Above the main deck of the vessel is an approximately 26m (75ft) enclosed shelter deck in which is found space for a Work class remotely operated vehicle (ROV), specialized machinery and various control, testing, storage and workshop spaces. At the bow end of the main deck is an open working deck where cable machinery and trenching plows can be stored. Above the main deck is an upper platform deck where various plow equipment and control stations are located. There is also room for stowage, workshop and control containers, as well as several hydraulic equipment and cargo handling cranes. Under the main deck aft are the ship's engine spaces. The engine consists of a pair of main propulsion diesels coupled through reverse and reduction gears to propellers turning in Kort nozzles. Also located in the machinery spaces aft are the ship's service generators, switchboards, auxiliary machinery and the engine control room. For added thrust, the vessel is fitted with a combination of fully azimuthing and tunnel thrusters.

SPECIFICATIONS

Type:	*ocean survey ship*
Crew:	*63*
Displacement:	*13,716 tonnes (13,500 tons)*
Length:	*131.5m (431.43ft)*
Beam:	*21.5m (70.53ft)*
Draught:	*4.57m (15ft)*
Speed:	*17.5 knots*
Range:	*unknown*
Missiles:	*none*
Guns:	*2 x .5in machine guns*
Torpedoes:	*none*
Helicopters:	*none*
Aircraft:	*none*
Air Search Radar:	*none*
Surface Radar:	*NR 58 DGPS & NR 230 DGPS*
Fire Control Radar:	*none*
Propulsion:	*2 x diesels*

RFA SIR GALAHAD

The roles of the Sir Lancelot class landing ships are to transport troops, vehicles and equipment. To do this the vessels have doors and ramps at the stern and bow and internal ramps between decks, making them truly "drive through". They also have a crane forward of the superstructure for on/off loading equipment. They can carry aircraft on the helicopter pad behind the main superstructure and on the vehicle deck. They also have facilities to carry ammunition, repair vehicles and equipment. These vessels also have the capability of offloading directly onto a beach. To allow this they have a shallow draught (they are virtually flat bottomed) and two large anchors at the stern which they drop at sea before beaching and later use to pull themselves back out to sea. The ships are also capable of carrying mexifloats which can support military vehicles. All vessels have an aft flight deck capable of handling Sea King or Lynx helicopters, or in the case of *Sir Bedivere* a Merlin. Helicopters (including Chinooks) can also land on the vehicle deck, with the exception of *Sir Bedivere*, but the Chinook can only land when the ship is in port. The present vessel was built to replace the previous vessel of the same name lost in the Falklands conflict in 1982. The new Alternative Landing Ship Logistic (ALSL) vessels will replace *Sir Galahad*.

SPECIFICATIONS

Type:	*large landing ship*
Crew:	*49 (plus up to 537 troops)*
Displacement:	*31,496 tonnes (31,000 tons)*
Length:	*140.47m (460.85ft)*
Beam:	*20m (65.61ft)*
Draught:	*4.57m (14.99ft)*
Speed:	*18 knots*
Range:	*9600km (6000 miles)*
Missiles:	*none*
Guns:	*2 x 20mm*
Torpedoes:	*none*
Helicopters:	*none*
Aircraft:	*none*
Air Search Radar:	*none*
Surface Radar:	*none*
Fire Control Radar:	*none*
Propulsion:	*2 x diesels, 47,000shp*

HMS SOMERSET

The Type 23 Duke class frigates at present carry Lynx helicopters. However, in the near future they will be replaced by Merlin, which has the capacity to carry up to four homing torpedoes such as the Stingray or Mark 11 depth bombs. The anti-surface version is able to carry a range of air-to-surface missiles including sea-skimming anti-ship missiles. There are optional gun positions through removable windows, the starboard cargo door and the port crew door. In the anti-ship surveillance and tracking role, Merlin uses its tactical surveillance and over-the-horizon targeting radar to identify the positions of hostile ships and relay the data to the allied command ship. The aircraft has a state-of-the-art, integrated mission system, which processes data from an extensive array of on-board sensors, giving it an independent capability to search for, locate and attack submarine targets. It is this autonomous capability which makes Merlin unique among ASW helicopters. The aircraft and its mission system are managed by two computer systems, linked by dual data buses. The cockpit is designed for operation by a single pilot, with the autopilot allowing for hands-off flight for most of the mission. Merlin is normally flown by a crew of three: pilot, observer and aircrewman, who can all access the management computers.

SPECIFICATIONS

Type:	frigate
Crew:	185
Displacement:	4267 tonnes (4200 tons)
Length:	133m (436.35ft)
Beam:	16.1m (52.82ft)
Draught:	5.5m (18.04ft)
Speed:	28 knots
Range:	12,480km (7800 miles)
Missiles:	Harpoon SSM, Sea Wolf SAM
Guns:	1 x 4.5in, 2 x 30mm
Torpedoes:	4 x 324mm tubes
Helicopters:	1 x Lynx or EH101 Merlin
Aircraft:	none
Air Search Radar:	Plessey Type 996 (I), 3D
Surface Radar:	Plessey Type 996 (I), 3D
Fire Control Radar:	2 x Marconi Type 911
Propulsion:	4 x diesels, 52,300shp

HMS SOUTHAMPTON

This Sheffield class guided missile destroyer (Type 42 Batch 1/2) has as its main gun the Vickers 4.5in Mk 8 gun. Since the early 1990s, naval surface fire support capabilities have been limited to these small-calibre guns, which lack adequate range, accuracy and lethality. Targeting and fire control are still done manually, and the navy acknowledges that the communications links between fire support ships and their customers are inadequate. A growing threat from sea-skimming anti-ship missiles is forcing fire support ships to operate at ever-increasing ranges from shore, further limiting the utility of guns. Notwithstanding the claims of manufacturers, the accuracy of naval gunfire depends on the accuracy with which the position of the firing ship has been fixed. Navigational aids, prominent terrain features or radar beacons emplaced on the shore may be used to compensate for this limitation. Bad weather and poor visibility make it difficult to determine the position of the ship by visual means and reduce the observer's opportunities for locating targets and adjusting fire. Bad weather also might force the ship out to sea. If the ship is firing while under way, the line of fire in relation to the frontline may change. This could cancel the fire mission, because the long-range probable errors may endanger friendly forces.

SPECIFICATIONS

Type:	destroyer
Crew:	253
Displacement:	4166 tonnes (4100 tons)
Length:	125m (410.1ft)
Beam:	14.3m (46.91ft)
Draught:	5.8m (19.02ft)
Speed:	29 knots
Range:	6400km (4000 miles)
Missiles:	Sea Dart SAM
Guns:	1 x 4.5in, 2–4 x 20mm, 2 x Phalanx
Torpedoes:	2 x triple torpedo tubes
Helicopters:	1 x Lynx
Aircraft:	none
Air Search Radar:	Marconi/Signaal Type 1022
Surface Radar:	Plessey Type 996
Fire Control Radar:	2 x Marconi Type 909
Propulsion:	2 x gas turbines, 54,000shp

VIRAAT

The carrier *Viraat* was originally HMS *Hermes*. She was built by Vickers-Armstrong, Barrow-in-Furness, and laid down on 21 June 1944 as one of the Centaur class light fleet carriers. She was not launched until 16 February 1953, being laid up a further four years awaiting completion. Completed on 18 November 1959, in 1971 she was recommissioned as a commando carrier, and then in the late 1970s as an interim V/STOL carrier. After serving as the flagship of the Royal Navy's task force during the 1982 Falklands War, she was stricken on 1 July 1985. The *Hermes* was sold to India on 19 April 1986, and after a major refit at Devonport before transfer, and renamed INS *Viraat* (R22), she was commissioned into the Indian Navy on 12 May 1987. The current air group includes 12 or 18 Sea Harrier V/STOL fighters and seven or eight Sea King or Kamov "Hormone" anti-submarine warfare (ASW) helicopters. In emergencies, the *Viraat* can operate up to 30 Harriers. She is due for retirement by 2010 following an extensive modernization programme that began in 1999. India continues her attempts to build or acquire additional aircraft carriers, and there are ongoing discussions about the possible transfer of the Russian ship *Gorshkov*, probably refitted as a full-deck V/STOL carrier.

SPECIFICATIONS

Type:	aircraft carrier
Crew:	1550
Displacement:	29,159 tonnes (28,700 tons)
Length:	208.8m (685.03ft)
Beam:	27.4m (89.89ft)
Draught:	8.7m (28.54ft)
Speed:	28 knots
Range:	unknown
Missiles:	Sea Cat SAM
Guns:	2 x 40mm, 2 x dual 30mm
Torpedoes:	none
Helicopters:	7 x Sea King
Aircraft:	12 x Sea Harrier
Air Search Radar:	Marconi Type 996
Surface Radar:	Plessey Type 994
Fire Control Radar:	2 x Plessey Type 904
Propulsion:	steam turbines, 76,000shp

GIUSEPPE GARIBALDI

The flagship of the Italian Navy, the *Giuseppe Garibaldi* carrier can carry out anti-submarine warfare, command and control of naval and aero-naval forces, area surveillance, convoy escort, commando transportation and fleet logistic support. The ship can accommodate up to 18 helicopters, for example the Agusta Sikorsky SH-3D Sea King or the Agusta Bell AB212. Alternatively, the ship can accommodate 16 AV-8B Harrier II aircraft, or a mix of helicopters and Harriers. Her long-range surface-to-surface missile (SSM) system, the MBDA Otomat, is installed on the gun decks at the stern of the ship, two launchers on the port and two on the starboard side. The missile has active radar homing, is armed with a 210kg (462lb) warhead and has a range of 120km (75 miles). The MBDA Albatros surface-to-air missile (SAM) system provides short-range point defence. The Albatros eight-cell launchers are installed on the roof decks at the forward and stern end of the main island. The system uses the Aspide missile, which has a semi-active radar seeker and a range of 14km (8.75 miles). Forty-eight Aspide missiles are carried. Fire control for the Albatros is provided by three AESN NA 30 radar/electro-optical directors, which include infrared camera and laser rangefinder as well as the Alenia RTN 30X fire control radar.

SPECIFICATIONS

Type:	*aircraft carrier*
Crew:	*550 plus 230 aircrew*
Displacement:	*13,584 tonnes (13,370 tons)*
Length:	*180m (590.55ft)*
Beam:	*33.4m (109.5ft)*
Draught:	*6.7m (21.98ft)*
Speed:	*30 knots*
Range:	*11,200km (7000 miles)*
Missiles:	*Otomat SSM, Aspide SAM*
Guns:	*6 x 40mm*
Torpedoes:	*A290 or Mk 46*
Helicopters:	*18 x SH-3D Sea King*
Aircraft:	*16 x AV-8B Harrier*
Air Search Radar:	*SPS 768 (RAN 3L)*
Surface Radar:	*SPS 774 (RAN IOS)*
Fire Control Radar:	*3 x AESN NA 30, 3 x NA 21*
Propulsion:	*4 x gas turbines, 81,000shp*

LERICI

The *Lerici*'s command system integrates the tactical data system with the major platform and operational systems. It includes the following features: control and operation of the suite of sensors and weapons; control of the main and auxiliary propulsion systems; and integrated control of all internal and external communications, including the transfer of messages and mine countermeasures data from the tactical consoles. The Integrated Ship Communications System has been developed by CEA Technologies and allows the management of all mine countermeasures activities, including mission planning, minehunting, mine disposal and post-mission analysis. If manoeuvring during minehunting operations is being automatically controlled, the system controls the auxiliary propulsion system via the minehunter autopilot. This provides the ship with auto-track and auto-hover for effective mine countermeasures operations. This class of ship has proved popular with other nations. For example, in 1986 South Korea began construction of the Swallow/Chebi class minehunter, which was based on the Lerici class. The Swallow class minehunter had new types of sonar and mine countermeasure equipment that was expected to improve the navy's capability to locate and to eliminate minefields in international shipping lanes during wartime.

SPECIFICATIONS

Type:	*minehunter*
Crew:	*50*
Displacement:	*683 tonnes (672 tons)*
Length:	*52.5m (172.24ft)*
Beam:	*9.87m (32.38ft)*
Draught:	*2.95m (9.67ft)*
Speed:	*15 knots*
Range:	*4000km (2500 miles)*
Missiles:	*none*
Guns:	*1 x 20mm*
Torpedoes:	*none*
Helicopters:	*none*
Aircraft:	*none*
Air Search Radar:	*none*
Surface Radar:	*none*
Fire Control Radar:	*none*
Propulsion:	*1 x diesel*

LIBECCIO

This Maestrale class frigate is a multirole warship. Essentially the Maestrales are enlarged and much improved Lupo designs. The most notable difference is the larger hangar housing two helicopters and the more modern weaponry and sensors. Each ship in the class is equipped with infrared decoy flares as protection against hostile missiles. These comprise the AMBL-2A long-range decoy-launcher, capable of firing parachute-suspended sub-munitions. It complements the shorter-range Mk 2 AMBL-1B system, which is suitable for smaller warships. Decoy rounds are contained in 34-round Type C "suitcases", and a delayed-action mechanism ensures that the cloud is co-located with the chaff cloud. Each IR decoy burns for 30 seconds at an altitude of 15m (49.21ft). Laid down in August 1979, *Libeccio* was launched in September 1981 and commissioned in February 1983. The ship's main gun installed on the bow deck is the Otobreda 127mm gun which fires 32kg (70.4lb) rounds at a rate of 45 rounds per minute. The range of the gun is more than 15km (9.37 miles) against surface targets and 7km (4.37 miles) against airborne targets. Two Otobreda 40mm twin anti-aircraft guns fire 0.96kg (2.11lb) shells at a rate of 300 rounds per minute to a range of 4km (2.5 miles) for airborne targets and to 12km (7.5 miles) for surface targets.

SPECIFICATIONS

Type:	*frigate*
Crew:	*232*
Displacement:	*3251 tonnes (3200 tons)*
Length:	*122.7m (402.55ft)*
Beam:	*12.9m (42.32ft)*
Draught:	*4.2m (13.77ft)*
Speed:	*32 knots*
Range:	*9000km (6000 miles)*
Missiles:	*Otomat SSM, Aspide SAM*
Guns:	*1 x 127mm, 4 x 40mm, 2 x 20mm*
Torpedoes:	*Mk 46, Whitehead A184*
Helicopters:	*2 x AB 212 ASW*
Aircraft:	*none*
Air Search Radar:	*Selenia SPS 774 (RAN 10S)*
Surface Radar:	*SMA SPS 702*
Fire Control Radar:	*Selenia SPG 75, 2 x Selenia SPG 74*
Propulsion:	*2 x diesels, 50,000shp*

LUIGI DURAND DE LA PENNE

The MM *Luigi Durand De La Penne* (D560) and the second of this class of ship, MM *Francesco Mimbelli* (D561), were commissioned in 1993. The ships were constructed at Fincantieri's Riva Trigoso shipyard. They were both built to replace older vessels, but the construction of two additional units has been cancelled. They are multirole warships able to perform anti-air defence for protecting task forces and convoys, anti-submarine and anti-surface warfare operations, assistance during landing operations and coastal bombardment. The IPN 20 command and control system gathers information from the ship's sensors and communications and data networks in order to compile, maintain and display the tactical situation. The ship's surface-to-surface missile (SSM) system is the Otomat Mk 2. Four twin launchers are installed on the missile deck amidship between the two radar masts. The missile uses mid-course guidance and active radar homing to approach the target at high subsonic speed in sea-skimming mode. The ship is also equipped with the SM-2MR Tartar GMLS Mark 13 missile system for defence against medium-range airborne targets. The SM-2MR has semi-active radar guidance and a range of 70km (43.75 miles). The ships are to be fitted with the MBDA Milas anti-submarine missile system.

SPECIFICATIONS

Type:	destroyer
Crew:	400
Displacement:	5486 tonnes (5400 tons)
Length:	147.7m (484.58ft)
Beam:	16.1m (52.82ft)
Draught:	5m (16.4ft)
Speed:	31.5 knots
Range:	11,200km (7000 miles)
Missiles:	Otomat SSM, Aspide SAM
Guns:	1 x 127mm, 3 x 76mm
Torpedoes:	Whitehead A 290
Helicopters:	2 x AB 212 ASW
Aircraft:	none
Air Search Radar:	Selenia SPS 768 (RAN 3L)
Surface Radar:	SMA SPS 702
Fire Control Radar:	4 x Selenia SPG 775, 2 x SPG 51D
Propulsion:	2 x diesels, 55,000shp

MAESTRALE

The lead ship in the Maestrale class of frigates, she is armed with the Otomat 2 over-the-horizon ship-to-ship missile, which has a range of 100–180km (62–112 miles). Due to influences from the curvature of the earth, the detection systems on the attacking ship itself are limited to direct use within approximately 40km (25 miles). Therefore, to operate and effect the over-the-horizon ship-to-ship missile, either a surface ship or a shipborne helicopter must take the forward position to act as a midway station to transmit pertinent data, relating target information and flight information on the missile back to the attacking ship. The helicopter simultaneously transmits pertinent commands from the firing ship or the midway point to the missile in flight, allowing the missile to hit the target with precision. Surface-to-air missiles (SAMs) consist of the Aspide, basically a licensed version of the American Sparrow, which is employed as both an air-to-air and surface-to-air missile, and in the latter role it is launched from both ships and ground platforms. The AIM-7E Sparrow entered service in 1962 and was widely used as a standard for other variants such as the Sky Flash (United Kingdom) and Aspide. At present there are eight ships in this class, all being launched between 1982 and 1985.

SPECIFICATIONS

Type:	frigate
Crew:	232
Displacement:	3251 tonnes (3200 tons)
Length:	122.7m (402.55ft)
Beam:	12.9m (42.32ft)
Draught:	4.2m (13.77ft)
Speed:	32 knots
Range:	9600km (6000 miles)
Missiles:	Otomat SSM, Aspide SAM
Guns:	1 x 127mm, 4 x 40mm, 2 x 20mm
Torpedoes:	Mk 46, Whitehead A184
Helicopters:	2 x AB 212 ASW
Aircraft:	none
Air Search Radar:	Selenia SPS 774 (RAN 10S)
Surface Radar:	SMA SPS 702
Fire Control Radar:	Selenia SPG 75, 2 x SPG 74
Propulsion:	2 x diesels, 50,000shp

MINERVA

This class was built to replace the older corvettes of the DeCristofaro and Albatross classes. While designated frigates and performing many of their jobs, these ships are perhaps best described as large corvettes which undertake general patrol duties. Fitted for but not installed with Teseo SSMs, these ships are used mainly for patrol and escort duties. The main gun is the Otobreda 76mm model. The company's Super Rapid Gun Mount is a multirole weapon intended as an anti-missile, anti-aircraft (AA) weapon system with anti-ship and naval gunfire support (NGS) capability. The gun in the AA role can use special pre-fragmented ammunition. For surface roles, special types of armour-piercing ammunition are available. New technologies are incorporated in order to enhance system effectiveness, and the company has developed the 76/62 family of ammunition to increase the performance of the 76/62 guns in terms of blast, fragmentation and perforation effects against air and surface targets. The maximum firing range of this projectile is 20km (12.5 miles) (instead of 16km [10 miles] as for standard 76/62 ammunition), without loss in accuracy and payload. In addition, full compatibility with the 76/62 gun mount's ballistics and mechanical feeding system is ensured. *Minerva* was launched in 1987.

SPECIFICATIONS

Type:	corvette
Crew:	122
Displacement:	1305 tonnes (1285 tons)
Length:	86.6m (284.12ft)
Beam:	10.5m (34.44ft)
Draught:	3.2m (10.49ft)
Speed:	24 knots
Range:	5600km (3500 miles)
Missiles:	Otomat SSM, Aspide SAM
Guns:	1 x 76mm
Torpedoes:	Honeywell Mk 46
Helicopters:	none
Aircraft:	none
Air Search Radar:	Selenia SPS 774 (RAN 10S)
Surface Radar:	Selenia SPS 774 (RAN 10S)
Fire Control Radar:	Selenia SPG 76 (RTN 30X)
Propulsion:	2 x diesels

ORSA

The *Orsa* is a Lupo class frigate. There were originally four in the class: *Lupo, Sagittario, Perseo* and *Orsa*. However, they were joined by those of the the Lupo (Artigliere) class of light frigates, which were built by Fincantieri at its Ancona and Riva Trigoso shipyards. They were initially built for Iraq, but delivery was cancelled following the United Nations embargoes against that country in 1990. New weapons and communications systems were fitted to meet the requirements of the Italian Navy. MM *Artigliere* (F582), MM *Aviere* (F583) and MM *Granitiere* (F585), built at Ancona, were commissioned in 1994, 1995 and 1996 respectively. The third-of-class ship, MM *Bersagliere* (F584), commissioned in 1995, was built at the Riva Trigosa shipyard in Genoa. The ship's surface search radar is the Selenia SPS 774 and the navigation radar is the SMA SPN 703, both operating at I band. The Alenia RAN 10S air search radar operates at E and F bands and has a range of 150km (240 miles). The ship has four fire control radars. Two I and J band Alenia SPG 70 fire control radars are long-range systems for use with the NA 21 fire control system for the missiles and main gun. The Alenia SPG 74 short-range fire control radar is used for the Dardo and the 40mm guns. A DE 1160B active search-and-attack sonar is also fitted.

SPECIFICATIONS

Type:	*frigate*
Crew:	*194*
Displacement:	*2565 tonnes (2525 tons)*
Length:	*113.2m (371.39ft)*
Beam:	*11.3m (37.07ft)*
Draught:	*3.7m (12.13ft)*
Speed:	*35 knots*
Range:	*6800km (4250 miles)*
Missiles:	*Otomat SSM, Sea Sparrow SAM*
Guns:	*1 x 127mm, 4 x 40mm*
Torpedoes:	*Whitehead A224*
Helicopters:	*1 x AB 212 ASW*
Aircraft:	*none*
Air Search Radar:	*Selenia SPS 774 (RAN 10S)*
Surface Radar:	*SMA SPS 702, SMA SPQ2*
Fire Control Radar:	*2 x Selenia SPG 70, 2 x SPG 74*
Propulsion:	*2 x diesels, 50,000shp*

SAGITTARIO

Another Lupo class frigate, the *Sagittario* is fitted with an electronic warfare suite includes a radar warning system and jammer. The decoy system consists of two SCLAR 20 tube 105mm decoy launchers. The SCLAR launcher deploys chaff, infrared decoys or illuminating flares in confusion, distraction and seduction modes. The engines drive two shafts with controlled pitch propellers. The turbines provide a maximum speed of 35 knots and the diesel engines provide a speed of 20 knots. She carries the AB 212 helicopter made by Agusta of Italy. It is a licence-built version of the UH-1N Iroquois or Huey multirole helicopter. Its "Twin-Pac" turboshaft installation consists of two turbines driving a single output shaft, either being able to drive the rotor if the other fails. The turbines are mounted outboard of the main rotor mast with the nozzles carried side-by-side in a single housing. The fuselage is of all-metal, semi-monocoque construction with a short nose, extensive glazing (including "chin" windows for look-down visibility) around the cockpit, and doors on both sides. The cockpit is open to the main cabin, which has large, rearward-sliding doors on both sides. The main cabin can carry troops in jump seats or litters in fold-down racks. Landing gear is parallel skids on tubular struts with a tail skid at the end of the tail boom.

SPECIFICATIONS

Type:	frigate
Crew:	194
Displacement:	2565 tonnes (2525 tons)
Length:	113.2m (371.39ft)
Beam:	11.3m (37.07ft)
Draught:	3.7m (12.13ft)
Speed:	35 knots
Range:	6800km (4250 miles)
Missiles:	Otomat SSM, Sea Sparrow SAM
Guns:	1 x 127mm, 4 x 40mm
Torpedoes:	Whitehead A224
Helicopters:	1 x AB 212 ASW
Aircraft:	none
Air Search Radar:	Selenia SPS 774 (RAN 10S)
Surface Radar:	SMA SPS 702, SMA SPQ2
Fire Control Radar:	2 x Selenia SPG 70, 2 x SPG 74
Propulsion:	2 x diesels, 50,000shp

VITTORIO VENETO

The *Vittorio Veneto* is a purpose-built helicopter cruiser that followed from the design of the Andrea Doria class of the 1950s. The addition of a second deck gave her a much greater helicopter capacity. A large central lift is set immediately aft of the superstructure and two sets of fin stabilizers make her a very steady helicopter platform. She has gone through two major refits in 1981 and 1984 which have upgraded her weaponry and radars. She was also refitted in the late 1980s. Six 40mm guns in twin turrets were added, and the Terrier missiles were removed and replaced by 40 Standard SM1 and 20 ASROC (Anti-Submarine Rocket) missiles. Two SPG 55C standard fire control systems were added, as were four Otomat SSM launchers. Her previous role of Italian flagship was handed over to the carrier *Giuseppe Garibaldi* in 1995. As well as carrying AB 212 helicopters, she has the capacity to field Sea Kings. She is expected to be decommissioned in 2005, though her life may be extended pending developments regarding new Italian carriers that are currently in production, one being the so-called "new major vessel". Building work on the new vessel, which will be named the *Andrea Doria*, began at Fincantieri's shipyards in Riva Trigoso and Muggiano in July 2001 and the ship will be delivered in 2007.

SPECIFICATIONS

Type:	*helicopter cruiser*
Crew:	*557*
Displacement:	*9652 tonnes (9500 tons)*
Length:	*179.6m (589.23ft)*
Beam:	*19.4m (63.64ft)*
Draught:	*6m (19.68ft)*
Speed:	*32 knots*
Range:	*8000km (5000 miles)*
Missiles:	*Otomat SSM, SM-1ER SAM*
Guns:	*8 x 76mm, 6 x 40mm*
Torpedoes:	*ASROC, Mk 46*
Helicopters:	*6 x AB 212 ASW*
Aircraft:	*none*
Air Search Radar:	*Selenia SPS 768 (RAN 3L)*
Surface Radar:	*SMA SPS 702*
Fire Control Radar:	*4 x Selenia SPG 70, 2 x SPG 74*
Propulsion:	*2 x steam turbines, 73,000shp*

JACOB VAN HEEMSKERCK

The *Jacob Van Heemskerck* is the missile version of the Kortenaer class, giving up ASW helicopter facilities in favour of an area-defence missile. It is armed with the Sea Sparrow missile that provides the capability of destroying hostile aircraft, anti-ship missiles, and airborne and surface missile platforms with surface-to-air missiles (SAMs). The ship can also be used to detect missile launchings by a surface vessel utilizing the NSSMS surveillance radar capability. The NSSMS consists of a Guided Missile Fire Control System (GMFCS) Mk 91 and a Guided Missile Launching System (GMLS) Mk 29. The GMFCS is a computer-operated fire control system that provides automatic acquisition and tracking of a designated target, generates launcher and missile orders, and in the automatic mode initiates the firing command when the target becomes engageable. Although most of the NSSMS operations are carried out under automatic or semi-automatic conditions, the GMFCS permits operator intervention and override at any time. The GMLS is a rapid-reaction, lightweight launching system that provides on-mount stowage and launch capability of up to eight missiles. The GMLS responds to launcher position commands, missile orders, and control commands issued by the GMFCS. The NSSMS employs Sea Sparrow III missiles.

SPECIFICATIONS

Type:	air defence frigate
Crew:	197
Displacement:	3810 tonnes (3750 tons)
Length:	130.5m (428.14ft)
Beam:	14.6m (47.9ft)
Draught:	4.3m (14.1ft)
Speed:	30 knots
Range:	7520km (4700 miles)
Missiles:	Harpoon SSM, Sea Sparrow SAM
Guns:	1 x Goalkeeper, 2 x 20mm
Torpedoes:	Mk 46
Helicopters:	none
Aircraft:	none
Air Search Radar:	Signaal LW 08
Surface Radar:	Signaal ZW 06
Fire Control Radar:	2 x STIR 240, STIR 180
Propulsion:	2 x gas turbines, 51,600shp

ADMIRAL PANTELEYEV

Designed primarily as an anti-submarine warfare platform, with a long cruising range and underway replenishment capabilities, the Udaloy class, to which *Admiral Panteleyev* belongs, reflects design changes that addressed the shortcomings of the previous Krivak programme: the lack of helicopter facilities, limited sonar capabilities and light air defences. The Udaloy has two helicopter hangars with doors that serve as a ramp to the flight deck. The Udaloy's air defence system consists of eight Klinok launchers, plus AK-630 and AK-100 gun mounts. Following Udaloy's commissioning, designers began developing an upgrade package in 1982 to provide more balanced capabilities. The Project 1155.1 Fregat II Class Large ASW Ships (NATO Codename Udaloy II) is intended to be the Russian counterpart to the US Arleigh Burke class ships. The Udaloy II is modified by the replacement of the SS-N-14 by the SS-N-22, reflecting a change in emphasis from ASW to anti-shipping. Other changes include an improved self-defence capability with the addition of the gun and SAM systems. Powered by modern gas turbine engines, it is equipped with more capable sonars, an integrated air defence fire control system, and a number of digital electronic systems based on state-of-the-art circuitry.

SPECIFICATIONS

Type:	*guided missile destroyer*
Crew:	*296*
Displacement:	*8839 tonnes (8700 tons)*
Length:	*163.5m (536.41ft)*
Beam:	*19.3m (63.32ft)*
Draught:	*7.5m (24.6ft)*
Speed:	*30 knots*
Range:	*6400km (4000 miles)*
Missiles:	*SA-N-9 SAM, SS-N-22, SA-N-11*
Guns:	*2 x 100mm, 4 x 30mm*
Torpedoes:	*Type 53*
Helicopters:	*2 x Ka-27 Helix A*
Aircraft:	*none*
Air Search Radar:	*Strut Pair, Top Plate, 3D*
Surface Radar:	*3 x Palm Frond*
Fire Control Radar:	*2 x Eye Bowl*
Propulsion:	*4 x gas turbines, 60,000shp*

SOVREMENNY

The Sovremenny class is designed to engage hostile ships by means of missile attack, and to provide warships and transport ships with protection against ship and air attack. Intended primarily for anti-ship operations, it was designed to compliment anti-submarine warfare (ASW) Udaloy destroyers. The ships are similar in size to the US Navy's AEGIS-equipped missile cruisers, and are armed with an anti-submarine helicopter, 48 air defence missiles, eight anti-ship missiles, torpedoes, mines, long-range guns and a comprehensive electronic warfare system. The first Sovremenny class destroyer was commissioned in 1985. The ship is equipped with the Moskit anti-ship missile system with two quadruple launchers installed port and starboard of the forward island and set at an angle of about 15 degrees to the horizontal. The air defence system is the Shtil surface-to-air missile (SAM). Two Shtil systems are installed, each on the raised deck behind the two-barrelled 130mm guns fore and aft of the two islands. The ships are further equipped with 130mm guns and four six-barrel AK-630 artillery systems for defence. Anti-submarine defence is provided by two double 533mm torpedo tubes installed port and starboard, and two six-barrel anti-submarine rocket launchers, RBU-1000, with 48 rockets, and a Ka-27 or Ka-25 helicopter.

SPECIFICATIONS

Type:	guided missile destroyer
Crew:	344
Displacement:	8067 tonnes (7940 tons)
Length:	156m (511.81ft)
Beam:	17.3m (56.75ft)
Draught:	7.85m (25.75ft)
Speed:	32 knots
Range:	22,400km (14,000 miles)
Missiles:	SS-N-22 SSM, SA-N-7 SAM
Guns:	4 x 130mm, 6 x 30mm AA
Torpedoes:	Type 53
Helicopters:	1 x Ka-25B or 1 x Ka-27
Aircraft:	none
Air Search Radar:	Top Steer, Plate Steer, Top Plate
Surface Radar:	3 x Palm Frond
Fire Control Radar:	Front Dome, Kite Screech, Bass Tilt
Propulsion:	2 x steam turbines, 100,000shp

KUZNETSOV

This aircraft carrier supports strategic missile-carrying submarines, surface ships and maritime missile-carrying aircraft of the fleet. She is capable of engaging surface, subsurface and airborne targets. Superficially similar to American carriers, the design is essentially "defensive": supporting nuclear submarine bases. The lack of catapults precludes launching aircraft with heavy strike loads, and the air superiority orientation of the air wing is apparent. Originally designated Black-Com-2 class, then subsequently the Kremlin class, these ships were finally redesignated Kuznetsov class. Initially Western analysts anticipated that they would have a combined nuclear and steam (CONAS) propulsion plant similar to the *Kirov* battle cruiser. However, the class was in fact conventionally propelled with oil-fired boilers. The first unit was originally named *Tbilisi*, and subsequently renamed *Admiral Flota Svetskogo Soyuza Kuznetsov*. The *Admiral Kuznetsov* is now the only operational aircraft carrier in the Russian Navy. A variety of aircraft were tested on her. The first specially configured Su-25UT Frogfoot B, Su-27 Flanker and MiG-29 Fulcrum conventional jets landed on her deck in November 1989, aided by arresting gear. The Mig-29K completed test flights from the deck of the aircraft carrier, but was not selected for production.

SPECIFICATIONS

Type:	*aircraft carrier*
Crew:	*1960 + 626 air wing + 40 flag*
Displacement:	*68,580 tonnes (67,500 tons)*
Length:	*280m (918.63ft)*
Beam:	*35.4m (116.14ft)*
Draught:	*10.5m (34.44ft)*
Speed:	*30 knots*
Range:	*unknown*
Missiles:	*SS-N-19 SSM, SA-N-9 SAM*
Guns:	*8 x CADS-N-1, 6 x 30mm*
Torpedoes:	*none*
Helicopters:	*15 x Ka-27, 3 x Ka-29 AEW*
Aircraft:	*20 x Su-27K, 4 x Su-25*
Air Search Radar:	*Sky Watch, 3D*
Surface Radar:	*Top Plate, 2 x Strut Pair*
Fire Control Radar:	*4 x Cross Sword*
Propulsion:	*2 x gas turbines, 200,000shp*

PYTLIVYY

The Krivak I frigate was an entirely new design, initially believed in the West to be designed for offensive surface warfare. In reality, the class was intended primarily as a defensive ASW ship. The Krivak was designed as a less expensive and capable counterpart to the larger Kresta II and Kara classes, with which it originally shared the BPK designation. Sources all agree that the Krivak I series consisted of 19 units, with the first unit being completed in 1970, though there is a difference of views as to whether the final unit was completed in 1980 or 1982. And while there is agreement on the names of these units, there is further argument regarding construction chronology. For example, some sources suggest that the *Pytlivyy* was one of the earlier ships, completed in 1974, while others state that is was the last ship, completed in 1982. At least two, possibly three, Krivak I frigates were modernized between 1987 and 1994. Known in the West as MOD Krivak, different sources suggest that the Soviet designation was either Project No 1135.2 Mod or Project No 1135.6. This modification featured a new surface-to-surface missile (SSM) in place of the old ASW rocket launcher, along with improved electronics and sonars. It was planned for all Krivak-I units, but was scrapped on financial grounds.

SPECIFICATIONS

Type:	frigate
Crew:	200
Displacement:	3658 tonnes (3600 tons)
Length:	123.5m (405.18ft)
Beam:	14.3m (46.91ft)
Draught:	5m (16.4ft)
Speed:	32 knots
Range:	7360km (4600 miles)
Missiles:	SS-N-25, SA-N-4, SS-N-14
Guns:	2 x 100mm
Torpedoes:	Type 53
Helicopters:	1 x Ka-27 (on Krivak III)
Aircraft:	none
Air Search Radar:	Head Net, Top Plate, 3D
Surface Radar:	Don Kay, Palm Frond
Fire Control Radar:	2 x Eye Bowl, 2 x Owl Screech
Propulsion:	2 x gas turbines, 48,000shp

BALEARES

These ships are modified from the basic USS *Knox* class design with Spanish-built electronics and weapon systems. Where the aft helicopter facilities sit on US-built ships, this ship has an enhanced outfit of ASW weaponry. The guided missile frigates bring an anti-air warfare (AAW) capability to the frigate mission, but they have some limitations. Designed as cost-effective surface combatants, they lack the multi-mission capability necessary for modern surface combatants faced with multiple, high technology threats. The RUR-5 Anti-Submarine Rocket (ASROC) is a ballistic missile designed to deliver the Mk 46 Mod 5 torpedo to a water entry point. Navy surface ships employed the ASROC with two different payloads: either a nuclear depth charge or the Mk 44 or Mk 46 lightweight acoustic torpedo. The ASROC weapons were relatively small devices designed to fit inside the distinctive eight-cell box launcher found on almost all cruisers and destroyers. The torpedo is a very sophisticated weapon employing, for its time, state-of-the-art technology for the propulsion and guidance systems. The torpedo is about 2.43m (8ft) long, weighs about 273kg (600lb) and is also carried in tubes on escort ships. After water entry, the torpedo powers up and attacks a submarine using either passive or active sonar.

SPECIFICATIONS

Type:	*frigate*
Crew:	*253*
Displacement:	*4244 tonnes (4177 tons)*
Length:	*133.6m (438.32ft)*
Beam:	*14.3m (46.91ft)*
Draught:	*4.7m (15.41ft)*
Speed:	*28 knots*
Range:	*7200km (4500 miles)*
Missiles:	*Harpoon, SM-1MR SAM*
Guns:	*1 x 127mm, 2 x 20mm*
Torpedoes:	*Mk 46 Mod 5*
Helicopters:	*none*
Aircraft:	*none*
Air Search Radar:	*Hughes SPS-52A, 3D*
Surface Radar:	*Raytheon SPS-10*
Fire Control Radar:	*SPG-53B, SPG-51 C, RAN 12 L*
Propulsion:	*4 x steam turbines, 35,000shp*

PRINCIPE DE ASTURIAS

The *Principe de Asturias* aircraft carrier has been in service with the Spanish Navy since 1988. The layout of the ship was partly derived from the design of the US Navy's Sea Control Ship. It normally supports a maximum of 29 fixed- and rotary wing aircraft with up to 12 on deck and 13 aircraft in the hangar. In an emergency, though, a maximum of 17 aircraft can be stored in the hangar. The hangar deck itself is accessed by two flight deck lifts. The ship has four FABA Meroka Mod 2B close-in weapon systems (CIWS), with twelve-barrelled Oerlikon L120 20mm guns. The guns have a rate of fire of 1440 rounds per minute and a range of up to 2000m (6562ft). They are installed as follows: two on the stern deck and one each on the port and starboard side of the flight deck. The Meroka fire control system has tracking radar and an ENOSA thermal imager. A Mk 13 Mod 4 eight-cell launcher for the Harpoon anti-ship missile is also fitted. The ship's decoy system is the Super Rapid Bloom Offboard Countermeasures, Super RBOC. The six-barrel launchers can fire both chaff and flare cartridges up to a range of 4km (2.5 miles). The towed torpedo decoy is the SLQ-25 Nixie decoy. A hull noise and propeller suppression system reduces the ship's acoustic signature and increases the effectiveness of the acoustic countermeasures deployed.

SPECIFICATIONS

Type:	aircraft carrier
Crew:	600 plus 230 air wing
Displacement:	17,463 tonnes (17,188 tons)
Length:	195.9m (314.63ft)
Beam:	24.3m (79.72ft)
Draught:	9.4m (30.83ft)
Speed:	26 knots
Range:	10,400km (6500 miles)
Missiles:	Harpoon ASM
Guns:	4 x Mod 2B CIWS, 2 x 37mm
Torpedoes:	none
Helicopters:	10 x Sea King, 4 x AB 212, 2 x SH-60B
Aircraft:	6–12 x AV-8B
Air Search Radar:	Hughes SPS-52 C/D 3D
Surface Radar:	ISC Cardion SPS-55
Fire Control Radar:	1 x RAN 12L, 4 x VPS 2, 1 x RTN 1
Propulsion:	2 x gas turbines, 46,400shp

USS ANTIETAM

Modern US Navy guided missile cruisers perform primarily in a Battle Force role. Due to their extensive combat capability, these ships have been designated as Battle Force Capable (BFC) units. These multi-mission ships are built to be employed in support of Carrier Battle Groups, Amphibious Assault Groups, as well as inter-diction and escort missions. The Ticonderoga class, using the highly successful Spruance hull, was initially designated as a guided missile destroyer (DDG), but was redesignated as a guided missile cruiser (CG) on 1 January 1980. They were the first surface combatant ships equipped with the AEGIS Weapons System, the most sophisticated air defence system in the world. The AEGIS combat system in Ticonderoga class cruisers, and the upgrading of older cruisers, have increased the anti-aircraft warfare (AAW) capability of surface com-batants. The heart of the AEGIS system is the AN/SPY-1A radar, which automatically detects and tracks air contacts to over 320km (200 miles). The AEGIS Weapons System is designed to defeat attacking missiles and provide quick reac-tion, high firepower and jamming resistance to deal with the AAW threat expected to be faced by the Battle Group. *Antietam* was commissioned on 6 June 1987 and will be decommissioned in 2022.

SPECIFICATIONS

Type:	*guided missile cruiser*
Crew:	*344*
Displacement:	*10,116 tonnes (9957 tons)*
Length:	*172.8m (566.92ft)*
Beam:	*16.8m (55.11ft)*
Draught:	*9.5m (31.16ft)*
Speed:	*30 knots*
Range:	*9600km (6000 miles)*
Missiles:	*SLCM, Harpoon ASM, SM-2 SAM*
Guns:	*2 x 127mm, 2 x Phalanx, 2 x 25mm*
Torpedoes:	*Mk 46, Mk 50*
Helicopters:	*2 x SH-60B*
Aircraft:	*none*
Air Search Radar:	*SPS-49*
Surface Radar:	*SPS-55*
Fire Control Radar:	*SPQ-9*
Propulsion:	*4 x gas turbines, 80,000shp*

USS ARLEIGH BURKE

The *Arleigh Burke* was the first US Navy ship designed to incorporate shaping techniques to reduce radar cross-section to defeat enemy weapons and sensors. The ship is used in high-threat areas to conduct anti-air, anti-submarine, anti-surface and strike operations. All ships of this class have the AEGIS (the Greek word for shield) air defence system with the SPY-1D phased array radar. They are armed with a 90-cell Vertical Launching System capable of storing and rapidly firing a mix of Standard, Tomahawk and Vertically Launched ASROC (VLA) missiles. Other armament includes the Harpoon anti-ship missile, the 127mm (5in) gun with improvements that integrate it with the AEGIS Weapons System, and the Phalanx CIWS. AEGIS is designed to counter all current and projected missile threats. A conventional, mechanically rotating radar "sees" a target when the radar beam strikes that target once during each 360-degree rotation of the antenna. A separate tracking radar is then required to engage each target. In contrast, the computer-controlled AN/SPY-1D phased array radar of the AEGIS system brings all these functions together. The four fixed arrays send out beams of electromagnetic energy in all directions simultaneously, continuously providing a search and tracking capability for hundreds of targets at the same time.

SPECIFICATIONS

Type:	*guided missile destroyer*
Crew:	*323*
Displacement:	*8433 tonnes (8300 tons)*
Length:	*153.8m (504.59ft)*
Beam:	*20.4m (66.92ft)*
Draught:	*9.44m (31ft)*
Speed:	*32 knots*
Range:	*7040km (4400 miles)*
Missiles:	*SLCM, Harpoon ASM, SM-2 SAM*
Guns:	*1 x 127mm, 2 x Phalanx*
Torpedoes:	*Mk 46, Mk 50*
Helicopters:	*none*
Aircraft:	*none*
Air Search Radar:	*SPY-1D 3D*
Surface Radar:	*SPS-67(V)3*
Fire Control Radar:	*3 x Raytheon/RCA SPG-62*
Propulsion:	*4 x gas turbines, 100,000shp*

USS BARRY

The USS *Barry* is the second ship of the Arleigh Burke class. It is equipped with Tomahawk missiles, which are launched from her Mark 41 Vertical Launch System (VLS) – a multi-warfare missile launching system capable of firing a mix of missiles against airborne and surface threats. It is modular in design, with eight modules symmetrically grouped to form a launcher magazine. The modules contain all the necessary components for launching functions when interfaced with the AEGIS Weapons System. The 127mm gun, in conjunction with the Mark 34 Gun Weapon System, is an anti-ship weapon which can also be used for close-in air contacts or to support forces ashore with naval gunfire support. The AN/SQQ-89 integrated ASW suite is a very advanced anti-submarine warfare system. The AN/SQR-19 Tactical Towed Array Sonar (TACTAS) provides extremely long-range passive detection of enemy submarines, and the AN/SQS-53C hull-mounted sonar is used to actively and passively detect and locate submarine contacts. The ship also has the capability to land the SH-60B LAMPS Mark III helicopter, which can link to the ship for support in anti-submarine operations. These systems are supplemented by the SLQ-32V(2) electronic warfare suite, which includes passive detection systems and decoy countermeasures.

SPECIFICATIONS

Type:	guided missile destroyer
Crew:	323
Displacement:	8433 tonnes (8300 tons)
Length:	153.8m (504.59ft)
Beam:	20.4m (66.92ft)
Draught:	9.44m (31ft)
Speed:	32 knots
Range:	7040km (4400 miles)
Missiles:	SLCM, Harpoon ASM, SM-2 SAM
Guns:	1 x 127mm, 2 x Phalanx
Torpedoes:	Mk 46, Mk 50
Helicopters:	none
Aircraft:	none
Air Search Radar:	SPY-1D 3D
Surface Radar:	SPS-67 (V) 3
Fire Control Radar:	3 x Raytheon/RCA SPG-62
Propulsion:	4 x gas turbines, 100,000shp

USS BLUE RIDGE

USS *Blue Ridge* (LCC-19) was conceived in 1963 and was in the planning and design stage for four years. She was built by the Philadelphia Naval Shipyard in 1967 and commissioned on 14 November 1970. The *Blue Ridge* is the most capable command ship ever built, with an extremely sophisticated command and control system. The Joint Maritime Command Information System (JMCIS) consists of numerous powerful computers distributed throughout the ship, from which information and data from worldwide sources are entered into a central database. This single integrated database concentrates the available information into a complete tactical picture of air, surface and subsurface contacts, enabling the fleet commander to quickly assess and concentrate on any situation which might arise. This ability gives *Blue Ridge* a global command and control capability unparalleled in naval history. In addition to her sophisticated command and control system, an extremely refined communications system is also an integral part of the ship's design. Through an automated patch panel and computer-controlled switching matrix, any combination of communications equipment desired may be quickly connected. The "clean" topside area is intended to keep the ship's interference with her own communications system to a minimum.

SPECIFICATIONS

Type:	*amphibious command ship*
Crew:	*842*
Displacement:	*18,944 tonnes (18,646 tons)*
Length:	*194m (636.48ft)*
Beam:	*32.9m (107.93ft)*
Draught:	*8.8m (28.87ft)*
Speed:	*23 knots*
Range:	*20,800km (13,000 miles)*
Missiles:	*GMLS Mk 25 Mod 1 SAM*
Guns:	*4 x 76mm, 2 x Phalanx*
Torpedoes:	*none*
Helicopters:	*room for 1 utility helicopter*
Aircraft:	*none*
Air Search Radar:	*SPS-48C, 3D, SPS-40C, Mk 23 TAS*
Surface Radar:	*SPS-65(V)1*
Fire Control Radar:	*2 x Mk 51*
Propulsion:	*1 x geared turbine*

USS BOXER

Boxer is a Wasp class Landing Helicopter Dock (LHD), which are the largest amphibious ships in the world. Wasp class ships are the first to be specifically designed to accommodate the AV-8B Harrier jet and the LCAC hovercraft, along with the full range of US Navy and US Marine helicopters, conventional landing craft and amphibious assault vehicles to support a Marine Expeditionary Unit (MEU) of 2000 US Marines. They provide command and control and aircraft facilities for sea control missions, while operating with a Carrier Battle Group. They transport and land ashore not only troops, but also the tanks, trucks, jeeps, other vehicles, artillery, ammunition and various supplies necessary to support the amphibious assault mission. Monorail trains transport cargo and supplies from storage and staging areas throughout the ship to a well deck which opens to the sea through huge gates in the stern. There, the cargo, troops and vehicles are loaded aboard landing craft for transit to the beach. The well deck can be ballasted down for conventional craft to float out on their way to the assault area. Helicopter flights also transfer troops and equipment to the beach, while the ship's air traffic control capability simultaneously directs close air tactical support provided by aircraft and helicopter gunships.

SPECIFICATIONS

Type:	amphibious ship
Crew:	1108 plus 1894 US Marines
Displacement:	41,180 tonnes (40,532 tons)
Length:	257.3m (844.16ft)
Beam:	42.7m (140ft)
Draught:	8.1m (26.57ft)
Speed:	22 knots
Range:	15,200km (9500 miles)
Missiles:	Sea Sparrow SAM, RAM
Guns:	2 x Phalanx, 3 x 25mm
Torpedoes:	none
Helicopters:	42 x CH-46E Sea Knight
Aircraft:	6–8 x AV-8B Harrier
Air Search Radar:	SPS-48E, SPS-49 (V) 7
Surface Radar:	SPS-67
Fire Control Radar:	Mk 9
Propulsion:	2 x steam turbines, 70,000shp

USS BRIDGE

The mission of the fast combat support ship is to receive ammunition, provision, stores and petroleum products from shuttle ships, and to distribute them to the Carrier Battle Group ships while under way. The liquid cargo stowage includes 156,000 barrels of fuel, 500 barrels of lubrication oil, 20,000 gallons of cargo water, together with a cargo fuel control system. The dry cargo stowage includes cargo ordnance holds for 1829 tonnes (1800 tons) of ammunition, a refrigerated cargo hold and 800 bottles of gas. Additionally, there is special cargo accommodation for oversize items such as cable reels and canned jet engines. The ship is equipped with a comprehensive cargo transfer system with a dedicated cargo control centre. There are five fuel at sea (FAS) stations, six replenishment at sea (RAS) stations, four cargo booms and a vertical replenishment position for two helicopters. The electronic countermeasures suite is the AN/SLQ-32(V)3, which carries out surveillance, missile warning and countermeasures. When hostile signals are detected, for example, the processor compares the signal characteristics against a threat library in the computer's memory in order to identify the threat. In automatic mode, the system identifies a hostile threat and initiates the appropriate countermeasures.

SPECIFICATIONS

Type:	fast combat support ship
Crew:	667
Displacement:	49,276 tonnes (48,500 tons)
Length:	229.81m (754ft)
Beam:	32.61m (107ft)
Draught:	11.58m (38ft)
Speed:	25 knots
Range:	9600km (6000 miles)
Missiles:	Sea Sparrow SAM
Guns:	2 x Phalanx, 2 x 25mm
Torpedoes:	none
Helicopters:	3 x CH-46E
Aircraft:	none
Air Search Radar:	unknown
Surface Radar:	SPS-67
Fire Control Radar:	unknown
Propulsion:	4 x gas turbines, 100,000shp

USS CAPE ST GEORGE

This Ticonderoga class guided missile cruiser was commissioned on 12 June 1993. The Ticonderoga class brings a multi-warfare capability to US fleets which significantly strengthens battle group operational effectiveness, defence and survivability. The cruisers are equipped with Tomahawk cruise missiles, giving them additional long-range strike mission capability. The addition of Tomahawk in the CG-47 class has vastly complicated unit target planning for any potential enemy and returned an offensive strike role to the surface vessels that seemed to have been lost to air power at Pearl Harbor in 1941. Two 127mm gun mounts are used against threatening ships and boats, low-flying aircraft, or to bombard shore targets. In addition, the ships carry a strong anti-submarine warfare (ASW) suite and the navy's latest electronic warfare suite is also aboard. The cruisers have the most advanced underwater surveillance system available today. The ASW equipment consists of a hull-mounted sonar, an acoustic array sonar, which is towed like a tail behind the ship, and a helicopter that can locate ships or submarines over 161km (100 miles) away. These new cruisers have replaced older, less capable ships that are being taken out of service as part of the US Navy's overall plan to recapitalize the fleet.

SPECIFICATIONS

Type:	*guided missile cruiser*
Crew:	*344*
Displacement:	*10,116 tonnes (9957 tons)*
Length:	*172.8m (566.92ft)*
Beam:	*16.8m (55.11ft)*
Draught:	*9.5m (31.16ft)*
Speed:	*30 knots*
Range:	*9600km (6000 miles)*
Missiles:	*SLCM, Harpoon ASM, SM-2 SAM*
Guns:	*2 x 127mm, 2 x Phalanx*
Torpedoes:	*Mk 46, Mk 50*
Helicopters:	*2 x SH-60B*
Aircraft:	*none*
Air Search Radar:	*SPS-49(V)8*
Surface Radar:	*SPS-55*
Fire Control Radar:	*SPQ-9*
Propulsion:	*4 x gas turbines, 80,000shp*

USS CONSTELLATION

USS *Constellation*'s Combat Systems Suite is one of the most advanced and capable in the fleet. Mk 91 three-dimensional fire control, TAS missile targeting and SPS-49 long-range air search radar systems operate together to allow the ship's Tactical Action Officer to accumulate and assess all hostile contacts. Enhanced by worldwide satellite communications and high-frequency data links, information is available for anywhere at any time. Other state-of-the-art systems include the Aircraft Carrier Data system, Super High Frequency communications, Automatic Identification and Tracking, Joint Tactical Identification, and Positive Identification, Friend or Foe. The Electronic Chart Display and Information System (ECDIS) can show charts of most of the world's waterways with the simple click of a button. It automatically plots the ship's position by Global Positioning Satellite and keeps a complete record, alleviating yet another time-consuming job aboard ship. Also new to the ship is the Flat Panel Display. Seven such displays, strategically placed around *Constellation*'s bridge, give the crew instant access to every piece of ship control data available on one notebook-sized screen. The displays also make complex computations, such as course and speed for aircraft launches, automatically.

SPECIFICATIONS

Type:	aircraft carrier
Crew:	3150 plus 2480 air wing
Displacement:	83,081 tonnes (81,773 tons)
Length:	319.73m (1049ft)
Beam:	82.29m (270ft)
Draught:	11.58m (38ft)
Speed:	32 knots
Range:	19,200km (12,000 miles)
Missiles:	Sea Sparrow SAM
Guns:	3 x Phalanx
Torpedoes:	none
Helicopters:	8 x SH-3 G/H or SH-60F
Aircraft:	20 x F-14, 20 x F/A-18, 4 x EA-6B, 16 x A-6E, 4 x E-2C
Air Search Radar:	SPS-48 C/E, SPS-49(V)5, Mk 23 TAS
Surface Radar:	SPS-10F
Fire Control Radar:	3 x Mk 91

USS DWIGHT D. EISENHOWER

The *Dwight D. Eisenhower* is a Nimitz class nuclear aircraft carrier whose two nuclear reactors give her virtually unlimited range and endurance and a top speed in excess of 30 knots. Eight steam turbine generators each produce 8000 kilowatts of electrical power, enough to serve a small city. The ship has enough electrical generating power to supply electricity to a city of 100,000 and normally carries enough food and supplies to operate for 90 days. The carrier is capable of launching as many as four aircraft a minute, and her four catapults and four arresting gear engines enable her to launch and recover aircraft rapidly and simultaneously. In addition to their power-projection role, Nimitz class ships serve as joint command platforms in the worldwide command and control network. The carrier air wing can destroy enemy aircraft, ships, submarines and land targets. Aircraft are used to conduct strikes, support land battles, protect the battle group or other friendly shipping, and implement a sea or air blockade. The air wing provides a visible presence to demonstrate US power and resolve in a crisis. The ship normally operates as the centrepiece of a Carrier Battle Group consisting of four to six other ships, including guided missile cruisers, destroyers, frigates, replenishment ships and submarines.

SPECIFICATIONS

Type:	*aircraft carrier*
Crew:	*3200 plus 2480 air wing*
Displacement:	*92,950 tonnes (91,487 tons)*
Length:	*332.84m (1092ft)*
Beam:	*40.8m (133.85ft)*
Draught:	*11.3m (37.07ft)*
Speed:	*30 knots*
Range:	*unlimited*
Missiles:	*Sea Sparrow SAM*
Guns:	*3 x Phalanx*
Torpedoes:	*none*
Helicopters:	*8 x SH-3 G/H or SH-60F*
Aircraft:	*20 x F-14, 20 x F/A-18, 4 x EA-6B, 16 x A-6E, 4 x E-2C, 6 x S-3A/B*
Air Search Radar:	*SPS-48E, SPS-49(V)5, Mk 23 TAS*
Surface Radar:	*SPS-67V*
Fire Control Radar:	*3 x Mk 91*

USS ENTERPRISE

At her commissioning on 24 September 1960, *Enterprise*, the world's first nuclear-powered aircraft carrier, was the mightiest warship afloat. She is the longest carrier in the US Navy at 335.5m (1101ft) and also the tallest at 76.2m (250ft). She was built with a distinctive square island supporting phased-array radars and a complex electronic warfare (EW) system. Between 1979 and 1982 she was at Puget Sound Naval Shipyard receiving a reconstructed island and numerous improvements. When first completed, the island of the *Enterprise* had a very unique shaped structure consisting of a dome-shaped top resting on a box, supporting SPS-32 and 33 radars, plus many electronic countermeasures (ECM) antennas. These were all removed during retrofit, and the island was completely altered to resemble the island of Kitty Hawk class carriers. In January 1995 she returned to dock for upgrades to all of her combat and communications systems, intelligence suites, command and control capabilities, ventilation systems, berthing and dining areas, and underway replenishment equipment. USS *Enterprise* can carry up to 85 aircraft, and her annual operating cost is around $220,000,000 US. Upon her planned replacement by CVX-78 in 2013, she will have been in service for 52 years.

SPECIFICATIONS

Type:	aircraft carrier
Crew:	3350, air wing 2480
Displacement:	95,473 tonnes (93,970 tons)
Length:	335.5m (1101ft)
Beam:	80.77m (265ft)
Draught:	11.9m (39.04ft)
Speed:	33 knots
Range:	unlimited
Missiles:	Sea Sparrow SAM
Guns:	3 x Phalanx
Torpedoes:	none
Helicopters:	8 x SH-3 G/H or SH-60F
Aircraft:	20 x F-14, 20 x F/A-18, 4 x EA-6B, 16 x A-6E, 4 x E-2C, 6 x S-3A/B
Air Search Radar:	SPS-48E, SPS-49(V)5, Mk 23 TAS
Surface Radar:	SPS-67
Fire Control Radar:	3 x Mk 91

USS INGRAHAM

Uss *Ingraham* is one of 51 Oliver Hazard Perry class guided missile frigates. Frigates fulfil a protection of shipping (POS) mission as anti-submarine warfare (ASW) combatants for amphibious expeditionary forces, underway replenishment groups and merchant convoys. Perry class frigates are primarily undersea warfare ships intended to provide open-ocean escort of amphibious ships and convoys in low to moderate threat environments in a global war situation, though this is now unlikely since the demise of the Warsaw Pact. The ships are equipped to escort and protect Carrier Battle Groups, Amphibious Landing Groups, Underway Replenishment Groups and convoys. They can also conduct independent operations for counter-drug surveillance, maritime interception operations and exercises with other nations. The addition of Naval Tactical Data System, LAMPS helicopters, and the AN/SQR-18A(V) Tactical Towed Array System (TACTAS) has given these ships a combat capability far beyond the class programme expectations of the mid-1970s, and has made them an integral and valued asset in virtually any war-at-sea scenario. Armament includes the Phalanx CIWS, which is shown above. Ships of this class are often referred to as FFG 7 (pronounced "FIG 7") after the lead ship in the class, USS *Oliver Hazard Perry* (FFG 7).

SPECIFICATIONS

Type:	*guided missile frigate*
Crew:	*216*
Displacement:	*4166 tonnes (4100 tons)*
Length:	*138.07m (453ft)*
Beam:	*14.32m (47ft)*
Draught:	*7.65m (22ft)*
Speed:	*30 knots*
Range:	*7200km (4500 miles)*
Missiles:	*Harpoon ASM, SM-1MR SAM*
Guns:	*1 x 76mm, 1 x Phalanx*
Torpedoes:	*Mk 46*
Helicopters:	*2 x SH-60B LAMPS*
Aircraft:	*none*
Air Search Radar:	*SPS-49*
Surface Radar:	*SPS-55*
Fire Control Radar:	*Mk 92*
Propulsion:	*2 x gas turbines, 40,000shp*

USS JARRETT

This Oliver Hazard Perry class frigate was launched on 2 July 1983. The US Navy developed the FFG 7 class using the minimal manning concept, which means supervisors must accomplish all tasks with fewer people than larger ships. Below decks, two gas turbine engines provide power for propulsion that enables the ships to reach speeds in excess of 30 knots. These advanced propulsion units allow a ship to get underway quickly and rapidly change operating modes. The propulsion plant as well as the electrical power plant is computer controlled and monitored to ensure a smooth running and efficient system. The gas turbine engines can be started and be ready to come up to full power in five minutes. The Perry class was originally fitted with Raytheon's AN/SLQ-32(V)2, a self-defence electronic support measures (ESM) system offering limited frequency cover and questionable security. The SLQ-32 antennas in a Perry are carried at about 15.24m (50ft) above the waterline, providing an intercept range of only 37km (23 miles). Following the Iraqi Exocet attack on the USS *Stark* on 17 May 1987, it was decided to upgrade the (V)2 installation by adding a jammer codenamed "Sidekick". The new variant was later designated SLQ-32(V)5, and to date a number of (V)2s have been brought to the new standard.

SPECIFICATIONS

Type:	*guided missile frigate*
Crew:	*216*
Displacement:	*4166 tonnes (4100 tons)*
Length:	*138.07m (453ft)*
Beam:	*14.32m (47ft)*
Draught:	*7.65m (22ft)*
Speed:	*30 knots*
Range:	*7200km (4500 miles)*
Missiles:	*Harpoon ASM, SM-1MR SAM*
Guns:	*1 x 76mm, 1 x Phalanx*
Torpedoes:	*Mk 46*
Helicopters:	*2 x SH-60B LAMPS*
Aircraft:	*none*
Air Search Radar:	*SPS-49*
Surface Radar:	*SPS-55*
Fire Control Radar:	*Mk 92*
Propulsion:	*2 x gas turbines, 40,000shp*

USS JOHN C. STENNIS

The mission of USS *John C. Stennis* and her embarked air wing is to conduct sustained combat air operations while forward deployed in the global arena. Her two nuclear reactors give her virtually unlimited range and endurance and a top speed in excess of 30 knots. The ship's four catapults and four arresting gear engines enable her to launch and recover aircraft rapidly and simultaneously. The ship carries approximately three million gallons of fuel for her aircraft and escorts, and enough weapons and stores for extended operations without replenishment. USS *John C. Stennis* also has extensive repair capabilities, including a fully equipped aircraft intermediate maintenance department, a micro-miniature electronics repair shop, and numerous ship repair shops. The air wing can destroy enemy aircraft, ships, submarines and land targets, or lay mines hundreds of miles from the ship. Carriers usually operate in the centre of the battle group, with the surrounding ships providing outer defence. However, should aircraft or missiles penetrate this outer ring, USS *John C. Stennis* has Sea Sparrow short-range, surface-to-air missile (SAM) systems, the Phalanx close-in weapon system (CIWS) for cruise missile defence, and the SLQ-32 Electronic Warfare System. The ship cost $3.5 billion US, and her projected service life is 50 years.

SPECIFICATIONS

Type:	aircraft carrier
Crew:	3200 plus 2480 air wing
Displacement:	98,552 tonnes (97,000 tons)
Length:	332.84m (1092ft)
Beam:	78.33m (257ft)
Draught:	11.3m (37.07ft)
Speed:	30 knots
Range:	unlimited
Missiles:	Sea Sparrow SAM
Guns:	4 x Phalanx
Torpedoes:	none
Helicopters:	8 x SH-3 G/H or SH-60F
Aircraft:	20 x F-14, 20 x F/A-18, 4 x EA-6B, 16 x A-6E, 4 x E-2C, 6 x S-3A/B
Air Search Radar:	SPS-48E, SPS-49(V)5, Mk 23 TAS
Surface Radar:	SPS-67V
Fire Control Radar:	3 x Mk 91

USS JOHN F. KENNEDY

USS *John F. Kennedy* (CV 67) was named after the 35th President of the United States. The ship's keel was laid on 22 October 1964 at the Newport News Shipbuilding and Drydock Company in Virginia. President Kennedy's nine-year-old daughter Caroline christened the ship in May 1967 in a ceremony held at Newport News, and the ship subsequently entered naval service on 7 September 1968. *Kennedy* was originally designed as a CVA 67 attack aircraft carrier. In the early 1970s, however, the classification was changed to CV 67, indicating the ship was capable of supporting anti-submarine warfare aircraft, making it an all-purpose, multi-mission aircraft carrier. In September 1995, the USS *John F. Kennedy* became the Naval Reserve's first aircraft carrier. Homeported at Mayport, Florida, her primary function during contingency operations is to provide a surge capability, and in peacetime to support US Navy force training requirements. As with all other reserve ships, she remains fully mission ready. She completed a two-year comprehensive overhaul in the Philadelphia Naval Shipyard on 13 September 1995. Following the overhaul, she moved to her new homeport at the Mayport Naval Station in Mayport, Florida. She has also served as a test bed for the Cooperative Engagement Capability (CEC) programme.

SPECIFICATIONS

Type:	aircraft carrier
Crew:	3117 plus 2480 air wing
Displacement:	83,312 tonnes (82,000 tons)
Length:	320.6m (1051.83ft)
Beam:	76.8m (252ft)
Draught:	11.4m (37.4ft)
Speed:	32 knots
Range:	19,200km (12,000 miles)
Missiles:	Sea Sparrow SAM
Guns:	3 x Phalanx
Torpedoes:	none
Helicopters:	8 x SH-3 G/H or SH-60F
Aircraft:	20 x F-14, 20 x F/A-18, 4 x EA-6B, 16 x A-6E, 4 x E-2C
Air Search Radar:	SPS-48 C/E, SPS-49 (V) 5, Mk 23 TAS
Surface Radar:	SPS-10F
Fire Control Radar:	3 x Mk 91

USS KAUFFMAN

The *Kauffman* (FFG 59) is one of the so-called "long hull" Oliver Hazard Perry class frigates. Perry class ships were produced in two variants, known as "short hull" and "long hull", with the later variant being 2.43m (8ft) longer than the short hull version. The long-hull ships (FFG 8, 28, 29, 32, 33, 36–61) carry the SH-60B LAMPS III helicopters, while the short-hull units carry the less-capable SH-2G. A total of 55 FFG 7 Oliver Hazard Perry class ships were built, including 51 for the US Navy and four for the Royal Australian Navy. Of these, 33 are in active commissioned service and 10 are in the Naval Reserve Force (NRF). The "short hull" Perry class frigates are being retired at an advanced rate, even though they have 20 years left on their service life. The US Navy had hoped to phase out construction of this class with the 1983 ships, FFG 59 and 60, but the US Congress authorized (but did not fully fund) FFG 61 in 1984. The Naval Reserve currently operates 10 Oliver Hazard Perry class frigates. These ships maintain full readiness status and deploy with their Active Component counterparts when needed. One of their primary missions, which they fulfil simply by being available, is to make it possible for the Active Component to maintain its operating tempo at acceptable levels.

SPECIFICATIONS

Type:	*guided missile frigate*
Crew:	*216*
Displacement:	*4166 tonnes (4100 tons)*
Length:	*138.07m (453ft)*
Beam:	*13.71m (45ft)*
Draught:	*4.5m (14.76ft)*
Speed:	*30 knots*
Range:	*7200km (4500 miles)*
Missiles:	*Harpoon ASM, SM-1MR SAM*
Guns:	*1 x 76mm, 1 x Phalanx*
Torpedoes:	*Mk 46*
Helicopters:	*2 x SH-60B LAMPS*
Aircraft:	*none*
Air Search Radar:	*SPS-49*
Surface Radar:	*SPS-55*
Fire Control Radar:	*Mk 92*
Propulsion:	*2 x gas turbines, 41,000shp*

USNS KILAUEA

The ammunition ship's mission is the delivery of bombs, bullets, missiles, mines, projectiles, powder, torpedoes and various other explosive devices and incendiaries to the various ships in the fleet at sea. This type of support is necessary in order to achieve and maintain the US Navy's requirement for a high degree of logistical independence. The ships have four cargo holds, which break down into 14 magazines. A magazine is the level within the cargo hold, and is defined as a magazine due to the stowage of ammunition and the requisite fire-detecting and fire-fighting items found on each level. As well as their delivery of ordnance and other goods, these ships carry out a replenishment-at-sea capability for limited quantities of fuel, water and combat stores. The ships also have facilities for limited ship repair and maintenance services, as well as special project services. The four cargo holds are serviced by six high-speed cargo weapons elevators. The ships have a certified helicopter flight deck and can handle any US military helicopter as well as most commercial and allied helicopters. There are seven cargo transfer stations and one fuel delivery station. The ships can also receive fuel at sea from any of four stations, and there are four cargo booms which allow for shore or barge transfer.

SPECIFICATIONS

Type:	ammunition ship
Crew:	180
Displacement:	20,492 tonnes (20,169 tons)
Length:	171.9m (564ft)
Beam:	24.68m (81ft)
Draught:	9.44m (31ft)
Speed:	20 knots
Range:	unknown
Missiles:	none
Guns:	none
Torpedoes:	none
Helicopters:	2 x UH-46E
Aircraft:	none
Air Search Radar:	none
Surface Radar:	unknown
Fire Control Radar:	none
Propulsion:	1 x turbine, 22,000shp

USS KITTY HAWK

The USS *Kitty Hawk* is a conventionally powered aircraft carrier. Combined with the aircraft of Carrier Air Wing Five, it carries F-14, F/A-18, EA-6B, S-3 A/B, E-2CA aircraft and SH-3 or SH-60 helicopters, which gives it a multi-dimensional response to air, surface and subsurface threats. *Kitty Hawk* underwent two overhauls in the Bremerton, Wash., Naval Shipyard in 1977 and 1982. The ship's most significant maintenance period, however, was a Service Life Extension Program (SLEP) at the Philadelphia Naval Shipyard beginning from 1987 through 1991. That rigorous four-year overhaul added an estimated 20 years to the planned 30-year life of the ship. Over a three-month period in early 1998, nearly 4000 shipyard workers, sailors and contractors completed $65 million US in repairs (involving over 500 major jobs) in the Complex Overhaul of the dry-docked *Kitty Hawk*. All four of the *Hawk*'s screws were repaired (number three was replaced), and all the line shaft bearings were replaced. Containments were built around the shafts to maintain temperature and humidity levels while complex fibreglass work was completed. For the rudders, large holes were cut through the decks, and the rudders and all associated systems were removed. Refurbished rudders were then re-machined and installed.

SPECIFICATIONS

Type:	*aircraft carrier*
Crew:	*3117 plus 2480 air wing*
Displacement:	*87,376 tonnes (86,000 tons)*
Length:	*325.83m (1069ft)*
Beam:	*76.8m (252ft)*
Draught:	*11.4m (37.4ft)*
Speed:	*32 knots*
Range:	*19,200km (12,000 miles)*
Missiles:	*Sea Sparrow SAM*
Guns:	*3 x Phalanx*
Torpedoes:	*none*
Helicopters:	*8 x SH-3 G/H or SH-60F*
Aircraft:	*20 x F-14, 20 x F/A-18, 6 x S-3A/B 4 x EA-6B, 16 x A-6E, 4 x E-2C*
Air Search Radar:	*SPS-48 C/E, SPS-49 (V) 5, Mk 23 TAS*
Surface Radar:	*SPS-10F*
Fire Control Radar:	*3 x Mk 91*

USS LAKE ERIE

At the heart of this Ticonderoga class guided missile cruiser is the AEGIS combat system, which integrates electronic detection, command and decision programmes, and engagement systems. *Lake Erie*'s computer-controlled phased array radar eliminates the need for separate search and track radars by simultaneously performing both functions. The four fixed SPY radar arrays form small steerable beams of electromagnetic energy that provide almost instantaneous full radar coverage, capable of tracking hundreds of contacts at the same time. The engineering system aboard *Lake Erie* represents the latest technology in warship construction. Four LM-2500 gas turbine engines supply the ship with power, and are very similar to the engines that power the larger airliners used throughout the world. With all four engines on-line, 80,000 shaft horsepower is available to propel the ship. The Controlled Reversible Pitch Propellers optimize the ship's speed and manoeuvrability through the water. By varying the pitch and the revolutions per minute of the screws the ship can go from full ahead to a complete stop in two ship lengths. Electricity is supplied by three gas turbine generators, each one providing 2500kW of power to sustain the ship's functions. During operations, two generators are normally on-line.

SPECIFICATIONS

Type:	*guided missile cruiser*
Crew:	*344*
Displacement:	*10,116 tonnes (9957 tons)*
Length:	*172.8m (566.92ft)*
Beam:	*16.8m (55.11ft)*
Draught:	*9.5m (31.16ft)*
Speed:	*30 knots*
Range:	*9600km (6000 miles)*
Missiles:	*SLCM, Harpoon SSM, SM-2 SAM*
Guns:	*2 x 127mm, 2 x Phalanx, 2 x 25mm*
Torpedoes:	*Mk 46, Mk 50*
Helicopters:	*2 x SH-60B*
Aircraft:	*none*
Air Search Radar:	*SPS-49(V)8*
Surface Radar:	*SPS-55*
Fire Control Radar:	*SPQ-9*
Propulsion:	*4 x gas turbines, 80,000shp*

USS NASSAU

The primary war-fighting mission of the LHA 1 (Landing Helicopter Assault 1) Tarawa class is to land and sustain US Marines on any shore during hostilities. The ships serve as the centrepiece of a multi-ship Amphibious Readiness Group (ARG). Some 3000 sailors and US Marines contribute to a forward-deployed ARG composed of approximately 5000 personnel. The ships maintain what the US Marine Corps calls "tactical integrity": getting a balanced force to the same place at the same time. One LHA can carry a complete US Marine battalion, along with the supplies and equipment needed in an assault, and land them ashore by either helicopter or amphibious craft. This two-pronged capability, with the emphasis on airborne landing of troops and equipment, enables the US Navy and Marine Corps to fulfil their mission. Whether the landing force is involved in an armed conflict, acting as a deterrent force in an unfavourable political situation or serving in a humanitarian mission, the class offers tactical versatility. The Tarawa class is designed to operate independently or as a unit of a force, as a flagship, or individual ship unit in both air and/or surface assaults. To allow them to do this the vessels incorporate the best design features and capabilities of several amphibious assault ships currently in service.

SPECIFICATIONS

Type:	amphibious assault ship
Crew:	964 plus 1900 US Marines
Displacement:	40,564 tonnes (39,925 tons)
Length:	254.2m (833ft)
Beam:	40.2m (131ft)
Draught:	7.9m (25.91ft)
Speed:	24 knots
Range:	16,000km (10,000 miles)
Missiles:	RAM
Guns:	2 x Phalanx
Torpedoes:	none
Helicopters:	9 x CH-53D, 12 x CH-46D/E
Aircraft:	6 x AV-8B
Air Search Radar:	SPS-40, SPS-48E
Surface Radar:	SPS-67
Fire Control Radar:	Mk 23 TAS
Propulsion:	2 x steam turbines, 70,000shp

USNS NIAGRA FALLS

The mission of the Mars class combat stores ship is to conduct underway replenishment in support of US Navy operating forces by providing refrigerated stores, dry provisions, technical spares, general stores, fleet freight, mail and personnel by alongside or vertical replenishment means. To do this they are fitted with state-of-the-art replenishment-at-sea equipment. The Mars class combat stores ships are augmented by three T-AFS 8 Sirius class stores ships purchased from Great Britain (built in England in 1965 and 1966, they were extensively modernized with improved communications and underway replacement facilities). The ships of Military Sealift Command's (MSC's) Naval Fleet Auxiliary Force (NFAF) are the lifeline to US Navy ships at sea. *Niagra Falls* is part of the MSC Far East in the Western Pacific and Indian Oceans; to provide a combat-ready logistics force, sustained sealift, and special mission ships as required in support of unified and fleet commanders. *Niagra Falls* was commissioned on 29 April 1967. As well as this ship there are two others of the class currently in service: the *Concord* was commissioned on 27 November 1968, and the *San Jose* was commissioned on 23 October 1970. All ships were built by the National Steel and Shipbuilding Company.

SPECIFICATIONS

Type:	combat stores ship
Crew:	176
Displacement:	17,659 tonnes (17,381 tons)
Length:	177m (581ft)
Beam:	24m (79ft)
Draught:	8.53m (28ft)
Speed:	20 knots
Range:	unknown
Missiles:	none
Guns:	2 x Phalanx
Torpedoes:	none
Helicopters:	2 x UH-46
Aircraft:	none
Air Search Radar:	unknown
Surface Radar:	SPS-67
Fire Control Radar:	Mk 23 TAS
Propulsion:	3 x steam turbines, 22,000shp

USS NIMITZ

The lead ship of her class, the *Nimitz* has four aircraft elevators that bring aircraft to the flight deck from the hangars below. Small tractors spot the planes on the flight deck. Aviation fuel is pumped up from tanks below, and bombs and rockets are brought up from the magazines. Powerful steam catapults, nicknamed "Fat Cats", can accelerate 37-ton jets from zero to a safe flight speed of up to 288km/h (180mph) in about 91.5m (300ft) and in less than three seconds. The weight of each aircraft determines the amount of thrust provided by the catapult. When landing, pilots use a system of lenses to guide the aircraft "down the slope": the correct glide path for landing. The four arresting wires, each consisting of 50.8mm (2in) thick wire cables connected to hydraulic rams below decks, drag landing aircraft going as fast as 240km/h (150mph) to a stop in less than 122m (400ft). The "Air Boss" and his staff coordinate the entire operation, which is carefully monitored from the flight deck level as well as by the captain on the bridge. The functions of the flight deck crew are identified by the colours they wear: yellow for officers and aircraft directors; purple for fuel handlers; green for catapult and arresting gear crews; blue for tractor drivers; brown for chock and chain runners; and red for crash and salvage teams and the ordnance handlers.

SPECIFICATIONS

Type:	aircraft carrier
Crew:	3200 plus 2480 air wing
Displacement:	96,520 tonnes (95,000 tons)
Length:	332.84m (1092ft)
Beam:	76.8m (252ft)
Draught:	11.3m (37ft.07)
Speed:	30 knots
Range:	unlimited
Missiles:	Sea Sparrow SAM
Guns:	3 x Phalanx
Torpedoes:	none
Helicopters:	8 x SH-3G/H or SH-60F
Aircraft:	20 x F-14, 20 x F/A-18, 4 x EA-6B, 16 x A-6E, 4 x E-2C, 6 x S-3 A/B
Air Search Radar:	SPS-48E, SPS-49(V)5
Surface Radar:	SPS-67V
Fire Control Radar:	3 x Mk 91

USS OSCAR AUSTIN

This Arleigh Burke class guided missile destroyer is one of the ships in the class undergoing the Flight IIA upgrade, which includes the incorporation of embarked helicopters (SH-60R), an organic minehunting capability and the introduction of an area theatre ballistic missile defence capability to protect near coastal airfields and seaports. The first 28 Arleigh Burke class destroyers have a helicopter deck but no hanger or embarked helicopters. Ships in production Flight IIA, starting with USS *Oscar Austin*, also have landing and hangar facilities for the operation of two multi-purpose Light Airborne Multipurpose System (LAMPS) Mk III helicopters. The modifications require removal of the Harpoon missile capability. The addition of a helicopter hangar and the upgraded baseline AEGIS system are two of the most significant upgrades. Also beginning with this ship, the number of Vertical Launch System (VLS) cells will be increased from 90 to 96, and the Phalanx close-in weapon system will be replaced by vertical-launched Sea Sparrow missiles. The hangar will be large enough to accommodate up to two helicopters, support equipment, repair shops and store rooms. Modifications were also made for additional crew required for a helicopter detachment to deploy with the ship. The SM-2 surface-to-air missile (SAM) is shown above.

SPECIFICATIONS

Type:	*guided missile destroyer*
Crew:	*380*
Displacement:	*9364 tonnes (9217 tons)*
Length:	*156.3m (513ft)*
Beam:	*20.11m (66ft)*
Draught:	*9.44m (31ft)*
Speed:	*32 knots*
Range:	*7040km (4400 miles)*
Missiles:	*SLCM, Sea Sparrow, & SM-2 SAMs*
Guns:	*1 x 127mm, 2 x Phalanx*
Torpedoes:	*Mk 46, Mk 50*
Helicopters:	*2 x SH-60R LAMPS III*
Aircraft:	*none*
Air Search Radar:	*SPY-1D 3D*
Surface Radar:	*SPS-67(V)3*
Fire Control Radar:	*3 x SPG-62*
Propulsion:	*4 x gas turbines, 100,000shp*

USS OSPREY

The Osprey class ships are the world's largest Glass-Reinforced Plastic (GRP) ships and are the first US Navy ships designed solely for minehunting. The technique used to locate mines is by high-definition sonar and the mines are neutralized with a remotely controlled underwater vehicle. The ships have been designed with exceptionally low magnetic and acoustic signatures to protect against mine detonations during minehunting operations. The mission of the ships is to clear coastal and ocean waters, shore areas and harbours of pressure/contact, acoustic and magnetic mines using reconnaissance, classification and neutralization. The ship is equipped with an AN/SLQ-53 deep sweep mine countermeasures system including an AN/SQQ-32 Variable Depth Sonar. The AN/SQQ-32 is a variable-depth minehunting sonar system for the detection and classification of mines, and is deployed by winch from a well in front of the bridge. Detection is carried out using multiple ping processing. The detection range is increased by using a lower operating frequency. The computer-aided detection techniques include marking of mine-like sonar contacts with track buckets for further detailed search. Classification of targets is carried out using higher-frequency narrow beam acoustics to provide high-resolution echo and shadow imagery.

SPECIFICATIONS

Type:	minehunter
Crew:	51
Displacement:	905 tonnes (889 tons)
Length:	57.3m (187.9ft)
Beam:	11m (36ft)
Draught:	3m (9.9ft)
Speed:	12 knots
Range:	2400km (1500 miles)
Missiles:	none
Guns:	2 x 12.7mm
Torpedoes:	none
Helicopters:	none
Aircraft:	none
Air Search Radar:	none
Surface Radar:	SPS-64(V)9
Fire Control Radar:	none
Propulsion:	2 x diesels, 5600shp

USS PLATTE

Fleet oilers operate as a unit of an underway replenishment group, replenishing petroleum products and ordnance to the fleet at sea during underway replenishments (UNREPS). The oilers transport bulk petroleum and lubricants from depots to the ships of the battle group. The ships also transport and deliver limited fleet freight, mail and personnel to combatants and support units underway. The ships are simultaneously capable of providing three double-probe fuel rigs to port, and two single-probe fuel rigs to starboard. The number of navy manned fleet oilers has decreased as more and more Military Sealift Command ships, manned by a civilian crew and commanded by a civilian master, have assumed responsibilities for supplying deployed ships. The ships' fully automated two-boiler steam propulsion plant propel them at a sustained speed of 20 knots while carrying a load of 150,000 barrels of fuel and 635 tonnes (625 tons) of ordnance. Liquid cargo transfer is provided by STREAM (Standard Tensioned Replenishment Alongside Method) double-hose stations located on the port and starboard sides. There is one replenishment station located on each side to provide the capability to transfer cargo, fleet freight and personnel. The large flight deck (shown above) is designed for helicopter landings.

SPECIFICATIONS

Type:	fleet oiler
Crew:	230
Displacement:	36,576 tonnes (36,000 tons)
Length:	180.2m (591.5ft)
Beam:	26.82m (88ft)
Draught:	9.54m (31.3ft)
Speed:	20 knots
Range:	unknown
Missiles:	none
Guns:	2 x Phalanx, 2 x 25mm
Torpedoes:	none
Helicopters:	none
Aircraft:	none
Air Search Radar:	unknown
Surface Radar:	SPS-67
Fire Control Radar:	Mk 23 TAS
Propulsion:	2 x steam boilers, 24,000shp

USS PORTER

The *Porter* was commissioned on 10 March 1999 and is one of the newest Arleigh Burke class destroyers. They are specifically constructed from a survivability enhanced design that affords passive protection to personnel and vital systems. This design provides protection against underwater shock, nuclear air blasts, fragment incursions into vital spaces, radar detection, electronic countermeasures, gun and missile attacks and a Chemical, Biological and Radiological (CBR) attack. A comprehensive Collective Protection System guards against nuclear, chemical or biological agents. The damage control features and constructional design make the ships the most "survivable" surface ship in the world. Extensive top-side armour is placed around vital combat systems and machinery spaces. The bulkheads are constructed of steel from the waterline to the pilot house. The bulkheads are designed with double-spaced plate construction for fragment protection. The frontal plate causes fragments to break up and the back-up plate stops the fragments from causing further damage to the interior of the ship. The AEGIS combat system equipment rooms are protected by Kevlar shielding, and top-side weight is reduced by incorporating an aluminum mast. Acoustic, infrared, and radar signatures have also been reduced.

SPECIFICATIONS

Type:	*guided missile destroyer*
Crew:	*346*
Displacement:	*9347 tonnes (9200 tons)*
Length:	*153.8m (504.59ft)*
Beam:	*20.4m (66.92ft)*
Draught:	*9.44m (31ft)*
Speed:	*32 knots*
Range:	*7040km (4400 miles)*
Missiles:	*SLCM, Harpoon & SM-2 SAMs*
Guns:	*1 x 127mm, 2 x Phalanx, 2 x 25mm*
Torpedoes:	*Mk 46, Mk 50*
Helicopters:	*none*
Aircraft:	*none*
Air Search Radar:	*SPY-1D 3D*
Surface Radar:	*SPS-67(V)3*
Fire Control Radar:	*3 x SPG-62*
Propulsion:	*4 x gas turbines, 100,000shp*

USS PRINCETON

USS *Princeton* (CG 59) is the US Navy's first cruiser equipped with the AN/SPY-1B radar system, which will provide a significant improvement in the detection capabilities of the AEGIS Weapons System. This radar system incorporates significant advances over earlier radars, particularly in its resistance to enemy electronic counter-measures (ECM). With the SPY-1B radar and the ship's Mk 99 fire control system, the ship can guide its Standard Missile to intercept hostile aircraft and missiles at extended ranges. Anti-ship cruise missile capability is provided by Harpoon missiles, capable of striking surface targets at ranges beyond 104km (65 miles). The AN/SQR-19 tactical towed array system provides long-range passive detection of enemy submarines, while the hull-mounted AN/SQS-53B sonar can be used to detect and localize submarine contacts. Two LAMPS Mk III multi-purpose helicopters function as extensions of the ship to assist in both submarine prosecution and surface surveillance and targeting. In addition, the AEGIS system will be capable of providing a threat-wide defence against tactical ballistic missiles. In addition to fulfilling its traditional missions, *Princeton* is equipped for strike warfare using the vertically-launched Tomahawk land-attack cruise missile.

SPECIFICATIONS

Type:	*guided missile cruiser*
Crew:	*344*
Displacement:	*10,116 tonnes (9957 tons)*
Length:	*172.8m (566.92ft)*
Beam:	*16.8m (55.11ft)*
Draught:	*9.5m (31.16ft)*
Speed:	*30 knots*
Range:	*9600km (6000 miles)*
Missiles:	*SLCM, Harpoon, SM-2MR M*
Guns:	*2 x 127mm, 2 x Phalanx, 2 x 25mm*
Torpedoes:	*Mk 46, Mk 50*
Helicopters:	*2 x SH-60B*
Aircraft:	*none*
Air Search Radar:	*SPS-49(V)8*
Surface Radar:	*SPS-55*
Fire Control Radar:	*SPQ-9*
Propulsion:	*4 x gas turbines, 80,000shp*

USS SENTRY

Avenger class ships are designed as minehunter-killers capable of finding, classifying and destroying moored and bottom mines. The mine countermeasures (MCM) ship performs precise navigation and clears minefields by sweeping moored, magnetic and acoustic influence mines. The MCM class also conducts coordinated operations with airborne and other mine countermeasure forces. This is the largest US Navy minesweeper to date and the first MCM ships to be built in America in nearly 30 years. The last three MCM ships were purchased in 1990, bringing the total to 14 fully deployable, oceangoing Avenger class ships. These ships use sonar and video systems, cable cutters and a mine detonating device that can be released and detonated by remote control. The ships are constructed of wood covered with glass-reinforced plastic (GRP) sheathing. The *Sentry* is equipped with the AN/SLQ-37(v) Standard Magnetic/Acoustic Influence Minesweeping System. It consists of a straight tail magnetic sweep (M Mk 5A) combined with the A Mk 4(v) and/or A Mk 6(b) acoustic sweeps. The system can be configured several ways, including diverting the magnetic cable and/or the acoustic devices by using components of the AN/SLQ-38 mechanical sweep gear.

SPECIFICATIONS

Type:	*minehunter*
Crew:	*84*
Displacement:	*1382 tonnes (1360 tons)*
Length:	*68.3m (224ft)*
Beam:	*11.9m (39ft)*
Draught:	*3.4m (11.75ft)*
Speed:	*13.5 knots*
Range:	*unknown*
Missiles:	*none*
Guns:	*2 x 12.7mm*
Torpedoes:	*none*
Air Search Radar:	*none*
Surface Radar:	*SC Cardion SPS 55*
Navigation:	*SSN- 2V Precise Integrated Navigation System (PINS)*
Fire Control Radar:	*none*
Propulsion:	*4 x diesels*

USS SPRUANCE

USS *Spruance* is the first destroyer to be back-fitted with the MK 41 Vertical Launching System (VLS). This allows her to engage shore-based and naval surface targets at long range. In addition, state-of-the-art computer and satellite technology allow the ships of this class to launch up to 61 precision-guided Tomahawk cruise missiles at land targets as far away as 1120km (700 miles). For example, ships of this class fired a total of 112 Tomahawk cruise missiles into Iraq during Operation Desert Storm in 1991 against important targets. They have subsequently been used for pre-emptive strikes at the direction of National Command Authorities against both Iraq and Bosnia. These ships have traditionally had a major role in Naval Surface Fire Support for troops ashore, employing Harpoon anti-ship missiles and two 127mm (5in) guns (also used for air defence and shore bombardment). The Harpoon missile system is proven effective in engaging shipping at intermediate ranges. The two MK 45 lightweight 5in 54-calibre guns can throw a projectile over 19.2km (12 miles) with a firing rate of 20 rounds per minute. The 5in gun represents a major step forward in medium-calibre ordnance for the US Navy, and the result is a weapon which allows a single man in a control centre to fire a barrage of 20 shells without assistance.

SPECIFICATIONS

Type:	*destroyer*
Crew:	*382*
Displacement:	*9144 tonnes (9000 tons)*
Length:	*171.7m (563.32ft)*
Beam:	*16.8m (55.11ft)*
Draught:	*8.8m (29ft)*
Speed:	*33 knots*
Range:	*9600km (6000 miles)*
Missiles:	*SLCM, Harpoon, Sea Sparrow*
Guns:	*2 x 127mm, 2 x Phalanx*
Torpedoes:	*Mk 46*
Helicopters:	*2 x SH-60B LAMPS III*
Aircraft:	*none*
Air Search Radar:	*SPS-40E*
Surface Radar:	*SPS-55*
Fire Control Radar:	*SPG-60, SPQ-9A*
Propulsion:	*4 x gas turbines, 80,000shp*

USS STOUT

This Arleigh Burke class destroyer was commissioned on 13 August 1994. The design process for ships built at Ingalls Shipbuilding is accomplished using a three-dimensional computer-aided design (CAD) system, which is linked with an integrated computer-aided manufacturing (CAM) production network of host-based computers and localized minicomputers throughout the shipyard. The technology significantly enhances design efficiency, and reduces the number of manual steps involved in converting design drawings to ship components, improving productivity and efficiency. During the construction of a DDG-51 destroyer, hundreds of sub-assemblies are built and outfitted with piping sections, ventilation ducting and other shipboard hardware. These sub-assemblies are joined to form dozens of assemblies, which are then joined to form the ship's hull. During the assembly integration process, the ship is outfitted with larger equipment items, such as electrical panels, propulsion equipment and generators. The ship's superstructures are lifted atop the ship's midsection early in the assembly process, facilitating the early activation of electrical and electronic equipment. When hull integration is complete, the ship is moved over land via a wheel-on-rail transfer system, and onto the shipyard's launch and recovery drydock.

SPECIFICATIONS

Type:	*guided missile destroyer*
Crew:	*323*
Displacement:	*8433 tonnes (8300 tons)*
Length:	*153.8m (504.59ft)*
Beam:	*20.4m (66.92ft)*
Draught:	*9.44m (31ft)*
Speed:	*32 knots*
Range:	*7040km (4400 miles)*
Missiles:	*SLCM, Harpoon ASM, SM-2 SAM*
Guns:	*1 x 127mm, 2 x Phalanx, 2 x 25mm*
Torpedoes:	*Mk 46, Mk 50*
Helicopters:	*none*
Aircraft:	*none*
Air Search Radar:	*SPY-1D 3D*
Surface Radar:	*SPS-67(V)3*
Fire Control Radar:	*3 x SPG-62*
Propulsion:	*4 x gas turbines, 100,000shp*

USS TARAWA

The Tarawa class can fulfil a number of roles: flagship for embarked amphibious squadron, flag or general officer staff; aircraft carrier; amphibious assault launching platform, employing a variety of surface assault craft including the navy's Landing Craft Utility (LCU), and other amphibious assault vehicles; hospital ship with 17 intensive care beds, four operating rooms, 300 beds, a 1000-unit blood bank, full dental facilities and orthopedics, trauma, general surgery, and x-ray capabilities; command and control ship; and assault provisions carrier able to sustain embarked forces with fuel, ammunition and other supplies. The LHA's flight deck can handle up to 10 helicopters simultaneously, as well as the AV-8B Harrier aircraft. There is also a large well deck in the stem of the ship for a number of amphibious assault craft, both displacement hull and air cushion. The ships have an extensive command, communication and control suite. These electronic systems give the amphibious task force commander nearly unlimited versatility in directing the assault mission. The heart of the LHA's electronic system is a tactical amphibious warfare computer which keeps track of the landing force's positions after leaving the ship, tracks enemy targets ashore and directs the targeting of the ship's guns and missiles.

SPECIFICATIONS

Type:	amphibious assault ship
Crew:	964 plus 1900 US Marines
Displacement:	40,564 tonnes (39,925 tons)
Length:	254.2m (833ft)
Beam:	40.2m (131ft)
Draught:	7.9m (25.91ft)
Speed:	24 knots
Range:	16,000km (10,000 miles)
Missiles:	RAM
Guns:	2 x Phalanx
Torpedoes:	none
Helicopters:	9 x CH-53D, 12 x CH-46D/E
Aircraft:	6 x AV-8B
Air Search Radar:	SPS-40, SPS-48E
Surface Radar:	SPS-67
Fire Control Radar:	Mk 23 TAS
Propulsion:	2 x steam turbines, 70,000shp

USS TICONDEROGA

The lead ship of the Ticonderoga class of guided missile cruisers, she is equipped with two SH-2G Seasprite helicopters. The SH-2G Super Seasprite was originally developed in the mid-1950s as a shipboard utility helicopter. Utilizing a unique blade flap design on the main rotors, the aerodynamic action of the flaps allows the pilot to fly without the aid of hydraulic assistance. The SH-2G is configured specifically to respond to the Light Airborne Multi-Purpose System (LAMPS) requirement of the United States Navy. The LAMPS concept extends the search and attack capabilities of carrier and convoy escort vessels over the horizon through the use of radar/electronic support measures (ESM) equipped helicopters. Primary missions of the SH-2G are anti-submarine warfare (ASW) and anti-ship surveillance and targeting (ASST). Secondary missions include search and rescue, vertical replenishment, medical evacuation, communications relay, personnel transfer, surveillance and reconnaissance, post-attack damage assessment, and naval gunfire spotting. Armament systems consist of two search stores systems (sonobuoys and marine location markers), an external weapons/stores system for external fuel tanks or torpedoes, and a countermeasures dispensing system. The other ships in the class carry two SH-60B Seahawk helicopters.

SPECIFICATIONS

Type:	*guided missile cruiser*
Crew:	*344*
Displacement:	*10,116 tonnes (9957 tons)*
Length:	*172.8m (566.92ft)*
Beam:	*16.8m (55.11ft)*
Draught:	*9.5m (31.16ft)*
Speed:	*30 knots*
Range:	*9600km (6000 miles)*
Missiles:	*SLCM, Harpoon, SM-2MR M*
Guns:	*2 x 127mm, 2 x Phalanx, 2 x 25mm*
Torpedoes:	*Mk 46, Mk 50*
Helicopters:	*2 x SH-2G*
Aircraft:	*none*
Air Search Radar:	*SPS-49*
Surface Radar:	*SPS-55*
Fire Control Radar:	*SPQ-9*
Propulsion:	*4 x gas turbines, 80,000shp*

USS TRENTON

The Austin class of amphibious ships is configured as flagships to provide extensive command, control and communications facilities to support amphibious landings. In an amphibious assault, the ship would normally function as the Primary Control Ship that would be responsible for coordinating boat waves and vectoring landing craft to the beach. A secondary mission is evacuation and civilian disaster relief. Hundreds of tons of relief materials can be carried aboard and delivered to disaster victims within minutes of the ship's arrival on the scene. Her medical and dental facilities can provide limited hospitalization care, as well as out-patient treatment for hundreds of sick or injured. The ship has a large flight deck for helicopter operations and a well deck that carries amphibious landing vehicles. The ships can carry one LCAC, or one utility landing craft (LCU) boat, or four mechanized landing craft (LCM), and six CH-46D/E helicopters, or three CH-53D helicopters, and 900 troops. To facilitate the docking and loading of various-sized landing craft, the ship can ballast down in the water, thereby flooding the well deck to enable the landing craft to enter the well deck through the stern gate door. Once docked inside the well deck, troops, supplies and combat equipment can be loaded into amphibious boats and vehicles.

SPECIFICATIONS

Type:	amphibious assault ship
Crew:	420 plus 900 US Marines
Displacement:	17,520 tonnes (17,244 tons)
Length:	173.8m (570.2ft)
Beam:	25.6m (84ft)
Draught:	7.2m (23.62ft)
Speed:	21 knots
Range:	12,320km (7700 miles)
Missiles:	none
Guns:	2 x Phalanx, 2 x 25mm
Torpedoes:	none
Helicopters:	6 x CH-46D/E or 3 x CH-53D
Aircraft:	none
Air Search Radar:	SPS-40 B/C
Surface Radar:	SPS-60
Fire Control Radar:	none
Propulsion:	2 x steam turbines, 24,000shp

USS WASP

These ships provide the means to deliver, command and support all elements of a Marine Landing Force in an assault by air and amphibious craft. In carrying out their mission, the ships have the option of utilizing various combinations of helicopters, Harrier II (AV-8B) close air support jump jets and air cushion landing craft (LCAC), as well as conventional landing craft and assault vehicles. Off the landing beach, the ship can ballast more than 15,240 tonnes (15,000 tons) of sea water for trimming during landing craft launch and recovery operations in the well deck. Wasp class ships can also provide command and control and aircraft facilities for sea control missions, while operating with an Aircraft Carrier Battle Group. They transport and land ashore not only troops, but also tanks, trucks, jeeps, other vehicles, artillery, ammunition and various supplies necessary to support the amphibious assault mission. Air cushion landing craft can "fly" out of the dry well deck, or the well deck can be ballasted down for conventional craft to float out. Helicopter flights also transfer troops and equipment to the beach, while the ship's air traffic control capability simultaneously directs close air tactical support provided by embarked jet aircraft and helicopter gunships. The two steam propulsion plants are the largest in the US Navy.

SPECIFICATIONS

Type:	*amphibious ship*
Crew:	*1108 plus 1894 US Marines*
Displacement:	*41,180 tonnes (40,532 tons)*
Length:	*257.3m (844.16ft)*
Beam:	*42.7m (140ft)*
Draught:	*8.1m (26.57ft)*
Speed:	*22 knots*
Range:	*15,200km (9500 miles)*
Missiles:	*Sea Sparrow SAM, RAM*
Guns:	*2 x Phalanx, 3 x 25mm*
Torpedoes:	*none*
Helicopters:	*42 x CH-46E Sea Knight*
Aircraft:	*6–8 x AV-8B Harrier*
Air Search Radar:	*SPS-48E, SPS-49(V)7*
Surface Radar:	*SPS-67*
Fire Control Radar:	*Mk 91*
Propulsion:	*2 x steam turbines, 70,000shp*

INDEX